REVISE EDEXCEL GCSE (9–1)
Business

REVISION WORKBOOK

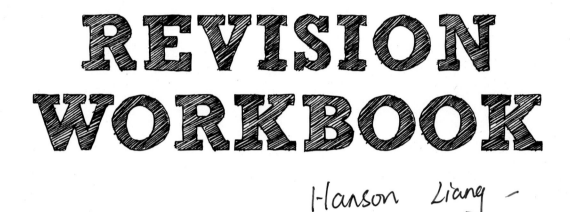

Hanson Liang

Series Consultant: Harry Smith

Author: Andrew Redfern

Also available to support your revision:

Revise GCSE Study Skills Guide   9781447967071

The **Revise GCSE Study Skills Guide** is full of tried-and-trusted hints and tips for how to learn more effectively. It gives you techniques to help you achieve your best – throughout your GCSE studies and beyond!

Revise GCSE Revision Planner   9781447967828

The **Revise GCSE Revision Planner** helps you to plan and organise your time, step-by-step, throughout your GCSE revision. Use this book and wall chart to mastermind your revision.

> **For the full range of Pearson revision titles across KS2, KS3, GCSE, Functional Skills, AS/A Level and BTEC visit:**
> www.pearsonschools.co.uk/revise

Contents

• •

A small bit of small print

Edexcel publishes Sample Assessment Material and the
Specification on its website. This is the official content and
this book should be used in conjunction with it. The questions
have been written to help you practise every topic in the book.
Remember: the real exam questions may not look like this.

The dynamic nature of business

1 Which one of the following is a reason for a product to become obsolete?

   Select **one** answer:

   ☐ **A** The product breaks

   ☐ **B** An accessory for the product is introduced

   ☐ **C** The product is unique

   ☑ **D** New technology is introduced   **(1 mark)**

2 Explain **one** way that changing consumer needs could create a new opportunity for a business.

   > Consumer needs may change due to shifts in lifestyle, fashion and economic conditions.

   For example , fashion has been changed. the business can change the lifest the clothes style to mee need the consumer.

   ....

   ....   **(3 marks)**

3 Explain **one** reason why a business owner might want to develop new ideas from existing products and services.

   Because it can make business more profit , less waste and grow business bigger.

   ....

   ....   **(3 marks)**

4 Discuss a factor that an entrepreneur should consider before opening a new business.

   Guided

   One factor that an entrepreneur may consider before opening a new

   business is whether or not there is a consumer need for the products

   or services that the business will offer. all of them

   for consumer that consumer could chase.

   ....

   ....

   ....

   ....   **(6 marks)**

Risk and reward

1 Which **one** of the following is a factor that could increase the level of risk in a business?

> **Guided**

Select **one** answer:

☐ **A**   Seasonal demand

☐ **B**   Having a large target market

☐ **C**   ~~Having low fixed costs~~

☐ **D**   Employing a large number of employees

> Having low fixed costs is an advantage for a business because it will need to sell fewer products before it starts to make a profit, so it does not increase risk.

(1 mark)

2 Explain **one** reason why running a business can involve high levels of risk.

> Think about the reasons why some businesses fail.

....

....

....

....

....

.... **(3 marks)**

3 Discuss a method that a business owner may use to reduce the level of risk in the running of their business.

> Research and planning are two ways that a business owner could reduce the risk. Write a detailed sentence explaining how good planning and good research could reduce risk.

....

....

....

....

....

....

....

....

....

....

.... **(6 marks)**

The role of business enterprise

1 Which **one** of the following is the purpose of a business?

Select **one** answer:

☐ **A** To produce goods and services

☐ **B** To minimise profit

☐ **C** To meet the needs of suppliers

☐ **D** To only work for the government   **(1 mark)**

> Guided

2 Which **one** of the following is **most** likely to be a customer for a marketing agency that produces brochures for tour operators?

Select **one** answer:

☐ **A** The public sector

☐ **B** The general public

~~☐ **C** The business that supplies the agency with paper~~

☐ **D** A business selling adventure holidays in Africa   **(1 mark)**

> It isn't option C because the business is a **supplier** not a **customer**.

3 Explain **one** way that a business can meet the needs of its customers.

....

....

....

....

....

....

....

....   **(3 marks)**

> Some customers buy products and services because they have a specific function or solve a certain problem. Often customers prioritise price over all other features, but they may also value quality and good customer service too.

The importance of added value

> Ellie Harrison owns the Witney Flower Shop, located in the high street in Witney, Oxfordshire. The business is established and successful. Ellie believes the success is the result of her unique selling point: Ellie imports exotic flowers such as orchids for her customers. No other flower shop in the area provides this service.

1 State the Witney Flower Shop's USP.

....

.... **(1 mark)**

2 Outline **one** method the Witney Flower Shop could use to add value to its products.

....

....

....

.... **(2 marks)**

3 Analyse the impact on the Witney Flower Shop of the business's location.

> Being located on a high street means the business is more visible to
>
> passing trade. This adds value because ....
>
> ....
>
> ....
>
> ....
>
> ....
>
> Furthermore, being located on a high street makes it easier for
>
> customers to visit the shop when buying from other local businesses.
>
> This adds value because ....
>
> ....
>
> ....
>
> ....
>
> .... **(6 marks)**

> **Guided**

The role of entrepreneurship

1 Which **one** of the following best defines the role of an entrepreneur?

Select **one** answer:

☐ **A** Someone who enjoys working in the service sector

☐ **B** Someone who wants to avoid paying income tax

☐ **C** Someone who owns and runs their own business and takes risks

☐ **D** Someone who runs a business while the owner is away on holiday   **(1 mark)**

2 Which **two** of the following are characteristics of an entrepreneur?

Select **two** answers:

☐ **A** A willingness to undertake a new venture

☐ **B** A very wealthy family background

☐ **C** A preparedness to take risks

☐ **D** Not willing to take financial risks

~~☐ **E** An education at least up to A-level~~   **(2 marks)**

> Guided

> It isn't option E because people do not need academic qualifications to be an entrepreneur.

3 Discuss an impact that entrepreneurs have on the economy.

....

....

....

....

....

....

....

....

....

....

....   **(6 marks)**

> The economy refers to society, people, businesses and the government. Select two of the following words to help you answer this question:
> • jobs
> • tax
> • exports
> • spending.

Customer needs 1

Samit Singh works as a bus driver for a local transport company in Stratford-upon-Avon. He is keen to start his own business providing an express bus service between Stratford-upon-Avon and Birmingham Airport. He spent a week doing market research. Samit interviewed 200 airport users in Stratford-upon-Avon town centre and some of the results are shown below.

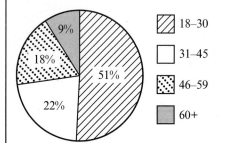

▨	18–30
☐	31–45
▨	46–59
▨	60+

Figure 1 Age profile of people who would use the service

Return fare	% of people prepared to pay
£14–£16	94%
£17–£18	76%
£19–£20	59%
£21–£24	31%
£25–£28	12%
£29+	3%

Table 1: The proportion of people interviewed prepared to pay different fares

1 Identify the percentage of people willing to pay **more than** £20.

....

.... **(1 mark)**

2 Identify the percentage of potential customers aged 46 or over.

....

....

.... **(1 mark)**

> The answer is not 18%. Take your time and look at the age brackets carefully.

3 Explain **one** reason why customer service is an important need that businesses should meet.

> Guided

Customer service is important because it is linked to the experience a

customer has when they buy a product ....

....

....

....

.... **(3 marks)**

Customer needs 2

Read the scenario about Samit on page 6.

Guided

1 Samit wants to differentiate his airport service from the services provided by rival businesses in order to attract customers. He is considering two options to achieve this.

Option 1: A discount of 20% for people who book more than one return trip in a year

Option 2: A door-to-door pick-up service for customers over the age of 60

> You could discuss one or both options in your answer. Show balance in your answer by analysing the benefits and limitations of at least one option. How can you link your answer to the market research?

Justify which **one** of these two options Samit should choose.

Option 1 may encourage customers to use Samit's service instead of

booking another service ....

....

....

....

....

....

> Decide which option is best and give a clear justification.

....

....

....

....

....

....

....

....

....

....   **(9 marks)**

The role of market research

A clothing shop wanted to find out about the views of its customers. Table 1 shows the results of a question asked to customers.

What is the major factor that attracts you to the shop?

	Number of responses
Value for money	28
Has the clothes that I want	36
Friendly staff	20
Well laid out	5
Late opening hours	11

Table 1

1 State **one** conclusion that the shop could draw from the customers' opinions listed in Table 1.

> What is the most important factor?
> What is the least important factor?

....

....

.... **(1 mark)**

2 Outline **one** appropriate method that the shop could use to anticipate its customers' needs.

....

....

....

.... **(2 marks)**

3 Explain **one** reason why a business would carry out market research.

> Guided

Market research can help a business to decide the price at which it

should sell its products ....

....

....

....

....

.... **(3 marks)**

Types of market research

1   Give **one** method of primary research.

....

.... **(1 mark)**

2   Explain **one** benefit to a business of using primary market research.

....

....

....

....

....

.... **(3 marks)**

> Primary market research is first-hand and conducted by the business, rather than by a third party.

3   Discuss the benefit of using secondary market research as opposed to other methods of research.

> When answering this question, you could:
> - discuss one benefit of secondary market research with several points of development
> - discuss two or more benefits of secondary market research with some points of development about each one.
>
> You could also discuss and develop a disadvantage of primary market research.

....

....

....

....

....

....

....

....

....

....

.... **(6 marks)**

9

Had a go ☐ Nearly there ☐ Nailed it! ☐

Market research data

1 Identify the sample size of customers surveyed by the clothing shop on page 8.

....

.... **(1 mark)**

2 Explain **one** reason why market research data might contain bias.

....

....

....

> **Bias** means that the people involved in the research are not impartial, which means that they are inclined to agree or disagree.

....

....

.... **(3 marks)**

3 Analyse a reason why the clothing shop on page 8 may also want to use a focus group to gather further market research.

> You may want to consider the following questions when you are planning your answer to this question.
> • What are the limitations of the current research carried out by the clothing shop?
> • How could using a focus group improve the quality of the research?
> • How could you refer to the qualitative data in your answer?

....

....

....

....

....

....

....

....

....

....

.... **(6 marks)**

Market segmentation

1 Give **two** possible ways in which a market could be segmented.

1 ....

....

2 ....

.... **(2 marks)**

2 Explain **one** limitation of market segmentation.

> Use the sentence structure below to give one reason and two linked strands of development.

Guided

One limitation of market segmentation is ....

....

....

This is because ....

....

As a result, ...

.... **(3 marks)**

3 Discuss **one** reason why a business may choose to target a specific segment of a market with its products and services.

> How might market segmentation make it easier for a business to:
> • develop products
> • advertise its products and services
> • conduct market research?

....

....

....

....

....

....

....

....

....

....

.... **(6 marks)**

Market mapping

Mario Tevez wants to open a restaurant specialising in South American cuisine. He thinks there might be a gap in the market in his home town of Odmoor in Yorkshire. Figure 1 is a market map that he has drawn up to identify whether there are any gaps in the market. There are currently eight restaurants in Odmoor.

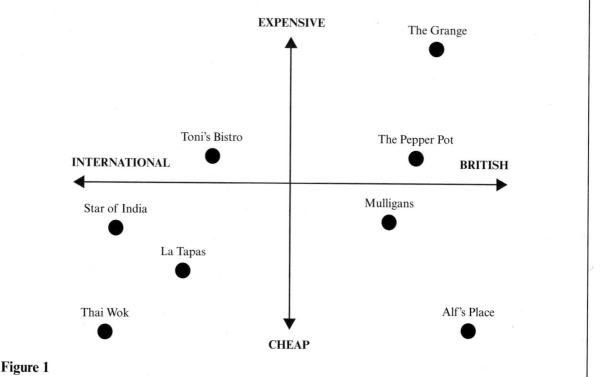

Figure 1

Mario is considering two options for the type of restaurant he would like to open in Odmoor.

Option 1: A premium-priced restaurant serving South American cuisine

Option 2: A medium-priced restaurant serving British cuisine

> Although it seems that there is a gap in the market for this type of restaurant, make sure you consider some of the limitations and issues Mario should bear in mind.

1   Justify which **one** of these options Mario should choose.

....

....

....

....

....

....

....

....

....

....

(9 marks)

Competition

> Valerie and Norman Trembath own a dairy farm in Cornwall. In 2015, they decided to use some of the milk they produced to make their own brand of ice cream. Their analysis of the local competition showed that there was only one supplier of premium-priced ice cream in the area, so they developed a brand called 'Truro's Best'. It is very rich and creamy, and it is sold at a premium price. Most of their customers are in the catering industry – hotels and restaurants. Valerie and Norman now have an established product range and can produce ice cream in any flavour ordered by their customers, which larger ice cream manufacturers cannot do.

1 State **one** reason why the Trembaths thought there was an opportunity in the local market for their premium ice cream.

....

.... **(1 mark)**

2 Outline **one** way in which the Trembaths have differentiated their ice cream.

> Add a point of development for the second mark in this question.

The Trembaths offer ice cream in any flavour ordered by customers.

....

....

....

....

.... **(2 marks)**

3 Outline **one** method that the Trembaths could use to further differentiate their ice cream.

> Differentiation is closely linked to adding value.

....

....

....

....

....

....

....

.... **(2 marks)**

Had a go ☐   Nearly there ☐   Nailed it! ☐

Competitive markets

Read the scenario about Valerie and Norman Trembath on page 13.

1 Explain **one** impact upon a business of increased competition in a market.

> If a large number of businesses sell a very similar type of product.

....

....

....

....

.... **(3 marks)**

2 Analyse an impact on the Trembaths' business if competitors entered the market.

> When answering this question, make sure that you:
> • explain at least one impact on Valerie and Norman's business
> • link your answer to the context of the scenario.

....

....

....

....

....

....

....

....

> What makes Valerie and Norman's ice cream stand out? How might this help them to beat the competition?

....

....

....

....

.... **(6 marks)**

Aims and objectives

Anna O'Neil had worked for a large supermarket chain for eight years and, by the age of 24, she wanted to run her own retail business. She was creative, driven and wanted to be her own boss. Her father lent Anna £40 000, plus she used £10 000 of her savings to open a shop. She chose to locate the shop in the town of Fort William in the Scottish Highlands, near Ben Nevis, in order to sell outdoor pursuits equipment and accessories. Her initial aim was to ensure that the business was still trading in two years' time.

After two years, Anna's business has started to make a small annual profit and has a strong cash-flow position. People such as climbers and skiers visit from all over Scotland, though usually only when visiting Ben Nevis and the surrounding area. The business has attracted publicity in national outdoor sports magazines because of its commitment to providing personal attention and advice for customers. It has also attracted a huge following on social media, where it shares pictures of its staff and customers climbing, skiing and mountain biking.

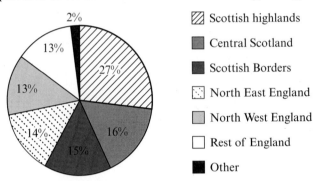

Scottish highlands
Central Scotland
Scottish Borders
North East England
North West England
Rest of England
Other

Figure 1 Where Anna's customers come from

Anna is now considering setting new objectives.

1 State **one** non-financial objective that Anna had when she launched her own business.

.... **(1 mark)**

2 Outline **one** non-financial objective that Anna's business could now adopt.

Guided ▶

Opening a second shop ....

....

.... **(2 marks)**

3 Explain **one** reason why a business owner might set an objective to break-even.

Why is it important to break-even?

....

....

....

....

.... **(3 marks)**

Had a go ☐   Nearly there ☐   Nailed it! ☐

Differing aims and objectives

Read the scenario about Anna on page 15.

1   Evaluate whether Anna should make her new aim to open a second shop. You should use the information provided as well as your knowledge of business.

When you are answering this question, you may include:
- a paragraph that analyses why this objective might be suitable, making at least two points about its suitability
- a paragraph that analyses why this objective might not be suitable, making at least two points about its unsuitability
- a justified decision, explaining what factors the decision may depend upon
- a recommended course of action for Anna to take, considering the factors that she should take into account.

....

....

....

....

....

....

....

....

....

....

....

....

....

....

....

....

....

....

....

.... **(12 marks)**

Use additional paper to complete your answer.

Revenues and costs

Philips is a small pottery business which specialises in ceramic plates. Table 1 contains financial information for one month (January).

Table 1

Number of ceramic plates produced and sold	200
Price per plate	£12
Variable cost per plate	£3
Fixed costs per month	£600

1 Calculate the total costs for Philips during the month of January. You are advised to show your workings.

£..

(2 marks)

2 Calculate the total revenue for Philips during the month of January. You are advised to show your workings.

> Guided

Revenue = Price × Quantity

£..

(2 marks)

3 Explain **one** reason why a business owner might want to reduce the variable cost per unit.

> The difference between the unit price and variable cost per unit is the profit margin (also known as the contribution).

....

....

....

....

....

....

....

(3 marks)

Had a go ☐ Nearly there ☐ Nailed it! ☐

Profit and loss

Philips is a small pottery business which specialises in ceramic plates. The owners would like to increase their profits, but they know that they are unlikely to increase their sales, so they are considering different options to increase profits. They would like to do this because the business made a loss last month.

1 State **one** action that Philips could take to increase their profits.

....

.... **(1 mark)**

2 Outline **one** reason why Philips may have made a loss last month.

....

....

....

.... **(2 marks)**

The owners of Philips are considering taking out a loan of £5000, which they will repay over four years. Their monthly repayment will be £116.50.

3 Calculate the total interest that Philips will pay for this loan as a percentage of the total amount borrowed. You are advised to show your workings.

> Give your answer to two decimal places.

......................................%

(2 marks)

4 The following table shows the costs, revenues and profits for Philips for a different two month period. Complete the table by filling in the **four** blanks.

> **Guided**

	June	July
Total revenue	£3000	£3200
Fixed costs	£600	£600
Variable costs	**(i)** £2200	**(iii)**
Total costs	£2800	**(iv)**
Profit/loss	**(ii)**	£500

> Total costs = Fixed + Variable costs
>
> Profit = Total revenue – Total costs

(4 marks)

Break-even charts

1 Which **one** of the following is a definition of the term 'break-even level of output'?

Select **one** answer:

☐ A ~~The level of output at which total profit = total costs~~

☐ B The level of output at which total fixed costs = total revenue

☐ C The level of output at which total variable costs = total fixed costs

☐ D The level of output at which total revenue = total costs   **(1 mark)**

> It isn't **A** because profit isn't used to calculate the break-even level of output.

Yffects is a small recording studio that offers bands and singers a chance to record an album. It has constructed the break-even chart shown in Figure 1. It charges customers £500 for a session to record their album.
- Its fixed costs are £4000.
- Variable costs are £250 a session.

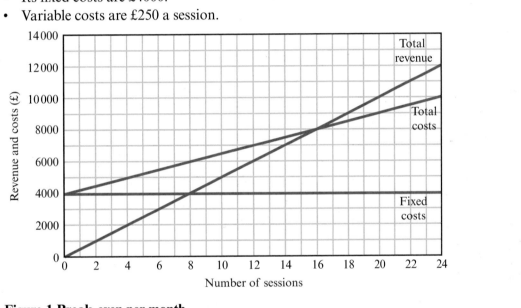

Figure 1 Break-even per month

2 Using Figure 1, identify the number of sessions that the business needs to sell in order to break even.

.... **(1 mark)**

3 Using Figure 1, identify the total revenue of the business if it sold 20 sessions a month.

.... **(1 mark)**

4 Using the information in Figure 1, calculate the profit if the business sold 24 sessions a month. You are advised to show your workings.

£..

> The profit for 24 sessions can be read from the chart by comparing the difference between the total costs and total revenue lines for 24 sessions and reading from the y-axis.

(2 marks)

Using break-even

> Yffects is a small recording studio that offers bands and singers a chance to record an album. It charges customers £500 for a session to record their album.
>
> • Its fixed costs are £4000.
> • Variable costs are £250 a session.

1 State **one** action that Yffects could take to increase its margin of safety.

> Guided

Reduce the fixed costs of ....

....

(1 mark)

Yffects thinks its price is too low compared with other studios. It has decided to increase its price to £570 per session.

2 Calculate the break-even level of output following this decision.

(2 marks)

3 Analyse the impact of Yffects using break-even analysis to make business decisions.

> It may help you to identify the different impacts of a decision if you remember that the impacts could be negative or positive.

....

....

....

....

....

....

....

....

....

....

....

(6 marks)

Calculating cash-flow

> Tees is a small business that prints T-shirts with designs on the front. In January, it had the following cash-flow information.
>
> Opening balance   £18 000
>
> Cash inflow   £17 000
>
> Cash outflow   £21 000

1   Calculate the net cash flow for Tees at the end of January. You are advised to show your workings.

> Net cash flow = Inflow – Outflow

£..

(2 marks)

2   Calculate the closing balance for Tees at the end of January. You are advised to show your workings.

£..

(2 marks)

3   The business has the following figures in September, October and November. Complete the table with the **three** missing figures.

Guided

	Sept (£)	Oct (£)	Nov (£)
Cash inflow	12 000	**(ii)** 14 000	8000
Cash outflow	19 000	22 000	24 000
Net cash flow	**(i)**	−8000	−16 000
Opening balance	20 000	13 000	5000
Closing balance	13 000	5000	**(iii)**

To find the **cash inflow** here subtract **net cash flow** from **cash outflow**.

(3 marks)

The importance of cash to a business

1   Which **one** of the following is a cash outflow from a business?

Select **one** answer:

☐ **A**   Encouraging customer payment

☐ **B**   Sales revenue

☐ **C**   Receiving a bank loan

☐ **D**   Purchasing assets

(1 mark)

2   Explain **one** reason why a strong cash flow is important to a business.

> What could having a strong cash flow allow a business to do?

....

....

....

....

....

....   **(3 marks)**

> Jayston Printing is a company that prints posters, magazines and leaflets. It has recently bought some new machinery with a loan, but has had problems owing to late payment by customers.

Delaying payments to suppliers is one method of improving cash flow.

3   Analyse the impact on Jayston Printing of delaying its payments to its suppliers.

> Guided

> There must be at least five linked strands of explanation in your answer. You can analyse one or two impacts on the business, but your answer should relate to Jayston Printing.

Delaying payment would help to maintain a positive net cash flow ....

....

....

....

However, delaying payment would could affect Jayston Printing's

reputation because ....

....

....

....   **(6 marks)**

Short-term sources of finance

1   Give **one** method that a business could use to improve its cash flow.

....

.... **(1 mark)**

> Gurrinder is a sole trader who is a designer and decorator. Her business – Be Different – designs offices that will appear unusual and unique to customers. Gurrinder's business has a healthy cash flow and is doing well. She would like to increase advertising and set up a new website.

2   Outline **one** short-term source of finance that Gurrinder could use to finance her planned business activities.

Guided

Gurrinder could arrange an overdraft with her bank ....

....

....

....

....

.... **(2 marks)**

3   Explain **one** benefit to a business of using short-term sources of finance.

> Expenses that could be paid using short-term sources of finance might include paying wages, supplier invoices and utility bills.

....

....

....

....

....

....

....

.... **(3 marks)**

Long-term sources of finance

Gurrinder is a sole trader who is a designer and decorator. Her business – Be Different – designs offices that will appear different to customers. Her last job was making the inside of a computer design studio look like a computer. She wants to expand into designing shops, factories and even film sets. She knows this will not happen overnight and that she will need long-term sources of finance.

1   Outline **one** long-term source of finance that Gurrinder could use to finance her business growth.

> Try not to outline either of the long-term sources of finance suggested in question 2.

....

....

....

....

....

(2 marks)

2   Gurrinder is considering two options to finance the expansion of her business:

Option 1: Retained profit

Option 2: Crowd-funding

Justify which **one** of these two options Gurrinder should choose.

> Work with the positive and negative aspects of Option 1 that have already been given.

Retained profit is a good long-term source of finance because it does not need to be repaid ....

....

....

....

....

....

However, it is likely that the expansion of her business will require a large amount of investment. ....

....

....

....

....

....

(9 marks)

Limited liability

1   Which **one** of the following is a result of being a sole trader?

Select **one** answer:

☐   **A**   The owner is only liable for the money that they invest in the business

☐   **B**   The business has to repay all loans instantly

☐   **C**   The owner receives all of the business's revenue

☐   **D**   The owner is liable for all of the business's debts

(1 mark)

2   Which **two** of the following are benefits of operating as a sole trader?

Select **two** answers:

> Guided

☐   ~~**A**   The business owner can benefit from limited liability~~

> It isn't option A because sole traders have **unlimited liability**.

☐   **B**   The business owner is likely to face greater risk

☐   **C**   The business owner will have greater control of the business

☐   **D**   The business owner can take all the profits of the business

☐   **E**   The business owner can sell shares to raise money

(2 marks)

3   Discuss the likely benefits to a business of changing from a sole trader to a private limited company.

> What securities do the owners of private limited companies have that sole traders do not have?

....

....

....

....

....

....

....

....

....

....

....

....

(6 marks)

Had a go ☐   Nearly there ☐   Nailed it! ☐

Types of business ownership

1 Define the term 'private limited company'.

....

.... **(1 mark)**

2 Give **two** disadvantages of running a business as a sole trader.

| What are the limitations of being a small business? |

1 ....

....

2 ....

.... **(2 marks)**

3 Explain **one** reason why a business may choose to become a private limited company.

> **Guided**

> What can a private limited company do that a sole trader cannot do? Give a reason and then develop your explanation with two linked strands of development. These could be causes or consequences.

A private limited company can sell shares to other people known to

the owner of the business ....

....

....

....

.... **(3 marks)**

4 Discuss a reason why customers may trust a private limited company more than a sole trader.

....

....

....

....

....

....

....

....

....

....

.... **(6 marks)**

Franchising

> Happy Dog is a franchise operation providing pet services such as dog walking, pet grooming and pet care for absent pet owners. Sandie Robinson is an animal lover, and she also wants to start her own business. However, Sandie has never run her own business before and does not want to manage a high level of risk. She is considering taking out a franchise with Happy Dog, which costs £9995.

1 State **one** benefit to Sandie of buying a Happy Dog franchise.

....

.... **(1 mark)**

2 Sandie is considering two options to start up her own pet services business.

Option 1: Buy the Happy Dog franchise

Option 2: Set up her own business

Justify which **one** of these two options Sandie should choose.

> You could answer this question by:
> • explaining the benefits and downsides of buying a franchise, applying the details that you are given about the Happy Dog franchise
> • explaining the benefits and downsides of opening a new business.
> • writing a justified conclusion outlining what Sandie should do.

If Sandie opens a Happy Dog franchise she will receive lots of support

....

....

....

....

....

However, £9995 is a lot of money to invest in a new business ....

....

....

....

....

....

Overall, I believe that it is better for Sandie to ....

....

.... **(9 marks)**

Had a go ☐ Nearly there ☐ Nailed it! ☐

Business location

1 Give **three** factors a business might consider when choosing a location.

> What things might a business want to be near to or have easy access to? For example, how close is the proposed location to services like public transport?

1 ....

2 ....

3 .... **(3 marks)**

2 Explain **one** reason why it might be an advantage for a business to set up on a busy high street.

> Think about how a business's location might be linked to promotion and awareness.

Guided

The business will be noticed by lots of potential customers

....

....

....

....

....

.... **(3 marks)**

3 Discuss a factor that a business that exports its products should consider when choosing a location for its factory.

> You could choose to answer this question by explaining two different factors or by explaining one factor in a lot of detail.

....

....

....

....

....

....

....

....

....

....

....

....

.... **(6 marks)**

The marketing mix

1 Which **one** of the following relates to a business's ability to communicate with its customers?

Select **one** answer:

☐ **A** Price

☐ **B** Product

☐ **C** Promotion

☐ **D** Place

(1 mark)

2 Which **one** of the following relates to a business's choice to sell its products through a particular retail store?

> **Guided**

Select **one** answer:

☐ ~~**A** Price~~

☐ **B** Product

☐ **C** Promotion

☐ **D** Place

> A business's choice of retail store affects the business's ability to get its product to its customers; not the price of its product.

(1 mark)

Goalz is a small sports and fitness business that is creating an app for sports people. The app will be used on mobile devices such as smartphones and tablets, and it will help people to record their sporting activities and track their achievements against their aims.

Market research shows that there are similar apps already on the market, but Goalz intends to sell its app at a slightly lower price than other apps. The Goalz app will also calculate a person's recovery time after exercise and provide personalised information to help improve their performance, which other apps do not. Goalz will advertise its app in national sports magazines and sell its app through popular app stores such as the Apple® App Store.

3 Outline **one** element of the marketing mix that Goalz could use to promote its product.

> Remind yourself of the 4 Ps: Product, Price, Promotion and Place.

....

....

....

....

....

....

(2 marks)

Influences on the marketing mix

1 Explain **one** way that the marketing mix might be influenced by technology.

> Choose a specific element of the marketing mix and a specific type of technology to focus your answer and help provide examples.

....

....

....

....

....

....

....

....

(3 marks)

> Amy Wong is a party organiser. Her business – Parties Ltd – organises a wide range of parties for weddings, birthdays, anniversaries, office parties, Christmas and other social events in the Cheltenham area. The company finds party locations and organises catering, music, decoration, drinks, costumes, transport and any other service that is required by the client.

Price and promotion are two elements of the marketing mix.

Guided

2 Analyse how price and promotion are connected for Parties Ltd.

> Make sure that your answer is in the context of Parties Ltd.

Because Amy targets a specific segment of the party

organising market ....

....

....

....

....

....

....

....

....

....

....

....

....

(6 marks)

The business plan

1 Which **one** of the following is **most likely** to be included in a business plan?

   Select **one** answer:

   ☐ A A copy of the business's headed notepaper

   ☐ B A forecast of cash flow for the two shops

   ☐ C A record of the profits of the two shops

   ☐ D A list of names of customers in the shop   **(1 mark)**

2 Which **one** of the following is the **most likely** reason to produce a business plan?

   Select **one** answer:

   ☐ A To guarantee shops make a profit

   ☐ B To attract customers to the shops

   ☐ C To reduce the chance of the shops failing

   ☐ D To train new staff in the shops   **(1 mark)**

> A **business plan** is a plan
> for the development of a
> business, giving forecasts
> of items such as sales,
> profits, costs and cash flow.

3 Discuss a reason why a business owner might write a business plan.

> Who might read a business
> plan once it has been
> written? What decisions
> might they make based on
> the business plan?

   ....

   ....

   ....

   ....

   ....

   ....

   ....

   ....

   ....

   ....

   ....

   ....

   ....

   ....

   ....   **(6 marks)**

The nature of business planning

> Marcus is the managing director of Delicious Italia Ltd, a small chain of shops in the UK that sells food from Italy. There is an Italian café in each shop. He wants to open two new shops in London.
>
> In order to open the new shops, Marcus requires £30 000 to renovate the two locations that he has identified. Both locations are in the centre of London, surrounded by a wide variety of other delis and cafés.

Marcus is considering two options to open his new shops.

Option 1: Prepare a detailed business plan and seek a bank loan

Option 2: Try to raise additional share capital without preparing a business plan

1 Justify which **one** of these two options Marcus should choose.

> When answering this question, you could:
> • explain the benefits of one of the two options in the context of Delicious Italia Ltd
> • explain the drawbacks of your chosen option in the context of Delicious Italia Ltd
> • write a justified conclusion that outlines why you think Marcus should choose the option you have analysed.

Having a business plan will be important for the success of Marcus's

newly opened shops. Choosing Option 1 will help ....

....

....

....

....

....

....

However, having a business plan does not guarantee success ....

....

....

....

....

....

....

....

.... **(9 marks)**

Stakeholders

1 Which **one** of the following is **most likely** to be a disadvantage to a business of having stakeholders?

Select **one** answer:

☐ **A** Stakeholders can have different views

☐ **B** Stakeholders can have different skills

☐ **C** Stakeholders can work for the business

☐ **D** ~~Stakeholders can put money into the business~~   **(1 mark)**

> It isn't option D because this is a **benefit** of having stakeholders.

2 Which **two** of the following are **most likely** to be benefits to a café of placing chairs and tables in the street?

Select **two** answers:

☐ **A** The business might want to get suppliers from somewhere else

☐ **B** It increases the space available for people to sit in

☐ **C** Customers might be attracted as they can smoke outside

☐ **D** Rivals could reduce prices to compete against the business

☐ **E** People in wheelchairs might find it difficult to get past tables   **(3 marks)**

3 Draw lines to match each objective on the left with the relevant stakeholder on the right.

> You won't be asked to answer questions like this in your exam. This one is just for practice.

Objective	
Value for money	i
Good employment conditions	ii
High profits, to get a returns on their shares	iii
Collecting tax on business revenue	iv
Reliable payment for orders	v

Stakeholder	
A	Local community
B	Government
C	Workers
D	Supplier
E	Managers
F	Competitors
G	Customers
H	Owners

Stakeholder conflict

Guided

1 Which **one** of the following is **most likely** to be the key interest of a shareholder
   in a business?

   Select **one** answer:

   ☐ **A** The profit made by the business

   ☐ **B** Staff turnover

   ☐ **C** Employees' working conditions

   ☐~~ **D** Increasing employment opportunities for disadvantaged people~~   **(1 mark)**

   > Option D would be of interest to customers,
   > the government or charities working with
   > disadvantaged people, but it's unlikely to be the
   > most important interest for a shareholder.

> BHP Billiton is an Anglo-Australian multinational mining, oil and gas company. It is the world's
> largest mining company and made a profit of US$21.7 billion in 2011. In 2012, workers at some
> mines in Queensland, Australia went on strike in protest over their working conditions. They
> wanted an extra break for night-shift workers, and more family-friendly shifts. According to a
> management spokesman, the strikes were expected to affect supplies to customers.

2 State **two** other stakeholders (other than shareholders) in BHP Billiton.

   ....

   ....   **(2 marks)**

3 Outline **one** conflict that might exist between two of the groups of stakeholders
   in BHP Billiton.

   ....

   ....   **(2 marks)**

4 Analyse the impact on shareholders in BHP Billiton of conflict between
   employees and managers.

Guided

   > When answering this question, try to:
   > • consider the key interests of shareholders
   > • describe how these interests might be affected by strike action
   > • consider the long-term effects on sales.

   A shareholder's key interest in a business is the amount of money that

   they receive in return for their investment ....

   ....

   ....

   ....

   ....

   ....

   ....   **(6 marks)**

Technology and business

1   Give **two** types of technology that a business might use.

1   ....

2   ....   **(2 marks)**

2   Explain **one** disadvantage to a business of investing in new technology.

> **Guided**

One disadvantage is that employees have to be trained to

use the new technology ....

....

....

....

....

....   **(3 marks)**

> What might a business have to do to ensure new technology is integrated into the business and all employees know how to use it effectively?

3   Discuss the impact of technology on the marketing mix of a business.

....

....

....

....

....

....

....

....

....

....

....

....

....

....

....

....   **(6 marks)**

> Identify a specific technology and then explain how this could influence at least one of the 4 Ps.

Principles of consumer law

Mixon is a company that produces a range of vegetarian products for people aiming to lose weight. These include sugar substitutes, main meals, snacks, drinks and desserts. Its latest product is a quiche. The advertising for this new product uses the phrases:

- 'made only from natural ingredients'
- 'ideal for vegetarians'
- 'perfect as part of a diet for those looking to lose weight'
- 'ideal for a quick lunch'.

It has been suggested that the fat content of the quiche is only slightly lower than those of supermarket brands. Also, in one variety, a vegetarian alternative has been used instead of meat.

1   State **one** benefit to consumers of Mixon having to comply with consumer protection laws.

....   **(1 mark)**

2   Mixon is considering two options for the advertising for its new product.

Option 1: Using the advertising phrases suggested in the case study
Option 2: Choosing not to use the statements about weight loss and natural ingredients

Justify which **one** of these options Mixon should choose.

> When answering this question, you have to **justify** your decision. This means that you have to consider the advantages and disadvantages of your chosen option to Mixon.

....

....

....

....

....

....

....

....

....

....

....

....

....

....

....

....   **(9 marks)**

Principles of employment law

1 Explain **one** benefit to a business of adhering to health and safety regulations in its workplaces.

> When answering an 'explain' question, identify one benefit (or factor, reason or method) and then give two linked strands of development that may be a cause or a consequence of this benefit.

....

....

....

....

....

....

....

....

....   **(3 marks)**

2 Explain **one** limitation for a business of an increase in the minimum wage.

Guided

If the government increases the minimum wage, a business may have to

pay its workers more ....

....

....

....

....   **(3 marks)**

3 Discuss the impact on a business of failing to comply with recruitment legislation.

> What might a business do illegally when recruiting and employing workers? What consequences could this have on the business?

....

....

....

....

....

....

....

....

....

....   **(6 marks)**

37

Had a go ☐   Nearly there ☐   Nailed it! ☐

The economy and business

1 Define the term 'consumer income'.

.... **(1 mark)**

2 Which **two** of the following are the **most likely** reasons for a business to lower its prices?

Select **two** answers:

☐ **A** Competitors have raised prices

☐ **B** A fall in incomes of people who buy its products

☐ **C** ~~A rise in the price of raw materials~~

☐ **D** A fall in the supply of raw materials

☐ **E** Similar businesses entering the market   **(2 marks)**

> Option C would be more likely to cause a business to increase its prices.

3 Explain how rising consumer income might affect a business.

> When answering this question, you could:
> • state how rising consumer income would affect a business
> • develop two consequences of this effect, which could be linked to increasing demand and sales, the need for recruitment and increased profits.

....

....

....

....

....

....

....

....

.... **(3 marks)**

Unemployment and inflation

1 Which **one** of the following is used to measure unemployment in the UK? **(1 mark)**

Select **one** answer:

It isn't option C because the consumer price index is used to measure inflation.

☐ **A** The number of people in long-term unemployment

☐ **B** The number of people made redundant in a given month

☐ **C** The consumer price index

☐ **D** A monthly count of those people claiming unemployment benefit **(1 mark)**

2 Define the term 'unemployment'.

....

.... **(1 mark)**

3 Explain **one** impact of a low rate of inflation on a business.

Low rates of inflation will ensure that the prices charged by suppliers

will remain quite low and will not rise sharply ....

....

....

....

....

.... **(3 marks)**

Had a go ☐   Nearly there ☐   Nailed it! ☐

Interest rates

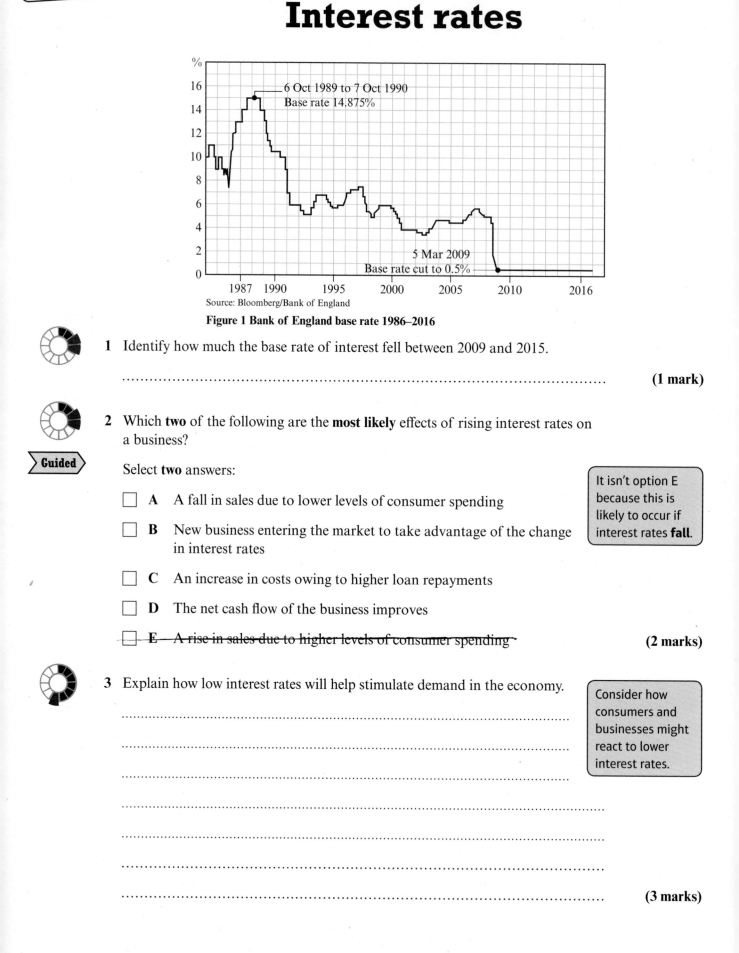

Source: Bloomberg/Bank of England

Figure 1 Bank of England base rate 1986–2016

1 Identify how much the base rate of interest fell between 2009 and 2015.

.... **(1 mark)**

2 Which **two** of the following are the **most likely** effects of rising interest rates on a business?

> **Guided**

Select **two** answers:

☐ **A** A fall in sales due to lower levels of consumer spending

☐ **B** New business entering the market to take advantage of the change in interest rates

☐ **C** An increase in costs owing to higher loan repayments

☐ **D** The net cash flow of the business improves

☐ **E** A rise in sales due to higher levels of consumer spending

(2 marks)

> It isn't option E because this is likely to occur if interest rates **fall**.

3 Explain how low interest rates will help stimulate demand in the economy.

....

....

....

....

....

....

(3 marks)

> Consider how consumers and businesses might react to lower interest rates.

Had a go ☐   Nearly there ☐   Nailed it! ☐

Exchange rates

1 Which **one** of the following is an example of an export for the UK?

Select **one** answer:

☐ **A** The sale of cars to Italy

☐ **B** The purchase of clothes from Bangladesh

☐ **C** The transfer of £25 000 from a UK bank account to a USA bank account

☐ **D** A visit by a UK school party to France   **(1 mark)**

2 Define the term 'exchange rate'.

....

.... **(1 mark)**

> The UK has a long history of trading with overseas nations. Today, for example, the UK sells whisky to the US, seafood to Spain, cars to Italy and pharmaceuticals to India. The UK also buys machinery from Germany, wine from Australia, vegetables from Peru and clothes from Bangladesh.

3 Analyse the impact of the strengthening of the pound against the US dollar on the profits of UK businesses exporting to the US.

Guided

> When answering this question, you may want to:
> • outline the effect on the prices of exports of the strengthening pound
> • explain the effect of USA demand for whisky resulting from the effect on the price of exports
> • explain how the change in USA demand will affect the profits of whisky producers in the UK.

If the pound becomes stronger against the US dollar, this means that

buyers in the USA must pay more for the whisky they buy from the UK

....

....

....

....

....

....

....

.... **(6 marks)**

External influences

1   Give **two** external influences that a business may have to consider.

   1   ....

   2   ....   **(2 marks)**

Guided

2   Explain **one** impact on UK businesses of a change in government legislation.

> You could consider a specific type of law to help think about the answer to this question.

   Changing legislation may affect UK businesses by making it

   harder for some businesses to trade ....

   ....

   ....

   ....

   ....

   ....

   ....

   ....   **(3 marks)**

3   Discuss the impact on businesses of the government encouraging people to use more renewable sources of energy.

> You could approach this question in two different ways:
> • Explain how businesses could see this as an opportunity.
> • Explain how businesses could see this as a threat.

   ....

   ....

   ....

   ....

   ....

   ....

   ....

   ....

   ....

   ....

   ....   **(6 marks)**

Exam skills: Case study

Answer ALL questions.
Look at Figure 1 and read the following extract carefully, then answer the questions.
Write your answers in the spaces provided.

In 2004, Cormac O'Donoghue started his own building business as a sole trader. Initially, he worked on small repair jobs, but he soon progressed to taking on house extensions and loft conversions. In 2010, Cormac set up Knight Construction Ltd and employed a small team of tradesmen including roofers, bricklayers and labourers. When he established the business, Cormac paid attention to his local competitors and positioned his business accordingly, as shown in Figure 1.

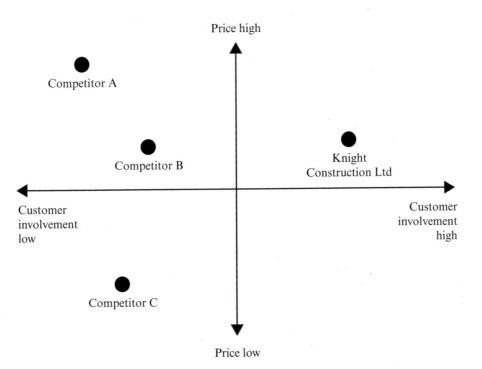

Figure 1

By 2016, Knight Construction Ltd had become one of the most reputable building companies in its area, with several teams of builders working on building projects throughout the year. The business benefits from positive word-of-mouth and personal recommendations that customers pass on to friends and family.

Cormac attributes the success of his business to the highly detailed quotes that they provide for their customers. The business also works hard to ensure that every project comes in on time and on budget, so that customers never have to pay more than their initial quotation. At times, the business absorbs costs to ensure that customers pay only what they were quoted. Knight Construction Ltd also allows its customers to spread their payments over the duration of the project, paying 50% of the final payment on the project's completion.

Cormac wants to improve the business's website and make it look more professional, so he intends to work with a web design business to develop a new website. The new website will feature time-lapse videos of projects that his company has completed for satisfied customers. In order to pay for the website development, Cormac intends to take out a £5500 loan from the bank with an interest rate of 8% per annum.

Exam skills: Practice paper

1 Using Figure 1, state a potential gap in the local market.

> Describe the quadrant on the market map where there are no competitors.

....

.... **(1 mark)**

2 Calculate the total repayment on the loan taken out by Knight Construction Ltd. You are advised to show your workings.

Guided

$$\frac{\text{Total repayment} - \text{Borrowed amount}}{\text{Borrowed amount}} \times 100 = \text{interest on loan (\%)}$$

5500 x 1.08 =

£...

(2 marks)

3 Outline **one** method that Knight Construction Ltd might use to promote its services other than word-of-mouth advertising.

> Identify one promotion method that would be suitable for a business like Knight Construction Ltd. You also need to provide a simple development of the method that you have identified.

....

....

....

....

....

....

.... **(2 marks)**

Guided

4   Outline **one** benefit to Knight Construction Ltd of using a market map.

What decisions can a market map help a business make?

Using a market map allows Knight Construction Ltd to

understand its competitors better ....

....

....

....

....

(2 marks)

5   Analyse the impact on Cormac's business of converting to a private limited company in 2010.

What protection would becoming a private limited company bring to Cormac's business?

....

....

....

....

....

....

....

....

....

....

....

....

....

....

....

....

....

....

....

....

(6 marks)

Guided

6 Analyse the impact on Knight Construction Ltd of allowing customers to spread payments over the duration of a project.

> Consider the positive and negative aspects of the impact. Will allowing customers to spread their payments make the business's services more attractive? What effect could this approach have on Knight Construction Ltd's cash flow?

This strategy enables Knight Construction Ltd to help its customers to manage their money more easily, which the business could promote as a USP ....

....

....

....

....

....

....

....

....

....

....

....

....

....

....

....

....

....

....

....

....

(6 marks)

Cormac is considering two options to improve the marketing mix of his business and attract more customers:

Option 1: Continue with his plans to increase marketing expenditure on his improved website

Option 2: Reduce his prices

> Guided

7 Justify which **one** of these two options Cormac should choose.

> A 'justify' question requires you to analyse the impact of one of two available options. You are then required to make a decision and support your decision with evidence. Your answer must be rooted in the context of the question.

By choosing Option 1 and making the business's website more professional, Knight Construction Ltd will support the promotion of the business ....

....

....

....

....

....

> Which of the 4 Ps (Product, Price, Promotion or Place) would the new website have an impact on? Could it have an impact on all four of them?

However, although the improved website will project a more professional image, it will not improve Knight Construction Ltd's marketing mix by itself ....

....

....

....

....

....

....

....

> In your answer, you might discuss the benefits and drawbacks of both options.

Overall, I think that Cormac should choose ....

....

....

.... **(9 marks)**

Due to economic influences and the rising cost of building materials, Cormac has estimated that his variable costs have increased by 15%.

Guided

8 Evaluate whether Cormac's decision to ensure that his customers do not pay more than their original quotation is a good decision. You should use the information provided as well as your knowledge of business.

> When answering this question:
> - Ensure your answer is in the context of Knight Construction Ltd and the building industry.
> - Explain the positive impact that ensuring every project comes in on budget will have on customer satisfaction, its reputation and the success of the company.
> - Explain the financial limitations of this decision and the impact it could have on the profitability of the business.
> - Discuss how this decision may depend on a range of other factors such as the extent of the cost and uncertainty of external factors.
> - Give a balanced decision with clear justification and recommendations.

Often building projects can exceed the initial quotation, meaning that many customers will worry about their finances when committing to a project such as a house extension or loft conversion. By doing its best to ensure this does not happen, Knight Construction Ltd will reassure customers, increase customer satisfaction and help to develop a good reputation in the local area ....

....

....

....

....

....

....

....

....

....

....

Overall, many customers will consider quality to be the most important factor when spending a lot of money on a new building and ....

....

....

.... **(12 marks)**

Use additional paper to complete your answer.

Business growth

1 Define the term 'takeover'.

....

.... **(1 mark)**

2 Explain **one** reason why a business would want to grow.

....

....

....

....

....

.... **(3 marks)**

3 Discuss a method that a business could use to grow internally.

> When answering this question, make sure that you:
> • choose one or more of the 4 Ps to talk about
> • explain an example of how your choice above might result in growth
> • discuss the first point with several strands of development or explain how changing a second P could also lead to growth.

....

....

....

....

....

....

....

....

....

....

.... **(6 marks)**

Public limited companies (PLCs)

> Snapchat is a popular messaging app used by millions of people. It was created by an American business called Snap Inc. In early 2017, the owners of Snap decided to float the business on the stock exchange and become a public limited company (PLC), with the intention of raising $3 billion of share capital. The business had never made a profit, but the popularity of Snapchat meant that it was widely expected to be valued at between $20 billion and $25 billion.

Snap Inc. could consider two options to raise funds.

Option 1: Sell 15% of the company through a stock market flotation

Option 2: Use crowd-funding

Guided

1   Justify which **one** of these two options Snap should choose.

> When answering this question, you could:
> • explain the benefits to Snap of becoming a PLC and selling shares publicly
> • discuss the limitations or dangers of stock market flotation
> • consider the short- and long-term issues
> • decide and justify whether this is the right decision for Snap.

Option 1 gives Snap the potential to raise considerable capital through

selling shares to the public ....

....

....

....

....

....

....

....

....

....

....

....

....

....

....

....

....

....   **(9 marks)**

Financing growth

1 Which of the following is an **internal** source of finance?

Select **one** answer:

☐ ~~**A**   A loan from the bank~~

It isn't option A because this
is from **outside** the business.

☐ **B**   A stock-market flotation

☐ **C**   Selling assets

☐ **D**   Venture capital

(1 mark)

2 Discuss the impact on a business of taking out a bank loan to finance business expansion.

....

....

....

....

....

....

....

(6 marks)

Pret A Manger is a sandwich and coffee shop chain that has grown considerably since it opened
its first shop in London in 1986. At the end of 2016, the chain had 444 shops around the world,
and in recent years it has expanded into countries such as France, China and the USA. In 2016,
Pret A Manger's sales in the USA exceeded $200m for the first time.

3 Analyse the impact on Pret A Manger of using retained profit to finance growth.

When answering this question, you could:
• discuss the benefits of financing growth with retained profit
• discuss the limitations of financing growth with retained profit
• ensure that your answer is applied to the Pret A Manger context.

....

....

....

....

....

....

....

....

(6 marks)

Why business objectives change

1 Which **one** of the following is an internal factor that may affect a business's objectives?

Guided

☐ **A** A new technology is introduced

☐ **B** The government introduces new employment legislation

☐ **C** The business appoints a new managing director

☐ **D** ~~A new competitor enters the market~~

> The entrance of a new competitor is an external pressure on the business.

(1 mark)

2 Explain **one** reason why competition may affect a business's choice of objectives.

....

....

....

....

....

....

(3 marks)

3 Discuss a reason why a business might have an objective to increase efficiency.

> Discuss at least one benefit that a business might get from improved efficiency and how this links to its objectives.

....

....

....

....

....

....

....

....

....

....

....

....

(6 marks)

How business objectives change

1 Which **one** of the following objectives is **most likely** to be adopted by a business intending to expand?

☐ **A** Improve efficiency

☐ **B** Maintain market share

☐ **C** Reduce costs

☐ **D** Open new stores **(1 mark)**

2 Explain **one** reason why market conditions can affect business objectives.

> Market conditions may be positive or negative. Choose one condition and then explain how this may affect a business's objectives.

....

....

....

....

....

....

.... **(3 marks)**

3 Discuss a reason why a business might set an objective to increase its product range.

> Guided

An objective to increase a business's product range could benefit the

business by appealing to a larger number of potential customers

....

....

....

....

....

....

....

....

....

....

....

.... **(6 marks)**

Business and globalisation

1 Define the term 'multinationals'.

....

.... **(1 mark)**

2 Explain **one** advantage of globalisation to an exporter.

> An exporter will look for opportunities to sell to international markets.

Globalisation is good for an exporter because it opens up

new markets to which they can sell ....

....

....

....

....

.... **(3 marks)**

3 Discuss the impact on small local businesses of increased levels of globalisation.

> You should approach this answer with a perspective.
> - Explain how small local businesses might benefit from globalisation.
> - Explain how small local businesses might be threatened by globalisation.

....

....

....

....

....

....

....

....

....

....

....

.... **(6 marks)**

International trade

1 Explain **one** advantage to a business of operating within a trade bloc.

....

....

....

....

....

.... **(3 marks)**

> Less economically developed countries (LEDCs) such as Kenya can benefit from international trade. For example, jobs might be created if an LEDC can export goods and services. One of Kenya's key exports is coffee.

2 Discuss the impact on businesses in Kenya of the UK placing a tariff on imports from foreign countries.

Guided

> You could approach this question by:
> • discussing how a tariff on Kenyan coffee could limit demand for the product in the UK
> • explaining the consequences for Kenyan coffee businesses and related trades
> • discussing how the tariff may have limited effect on Kenyan businesses, for example if they sell a lot of their coffee to other countries.

A tariff is a tax imposed by a country's government and levied on

imports into that country ....

....

....

....

....

However, Kenya may export much of its produce to other countries

that do not impose tariffs on imported goods such as coffee ....

....

....

....

....

....

.... **(6 marks)**

Had a go ☐   **Nearly there** ☐   **Nailed it!** ☐

Competing internationally

Guided

1   Which **one** of the following is a possible motive for imposing a tariff on imported goods?

Select **one** answer:

☐   A   ~~To increase imports~~

☐   B   To create a trade bloc

☐   C   To protect domestic businesses

☐   D   To decrease inflation

(1 mark)

> Imposing a tariff is likely to decrease imports, so it can't be Option A.

2   Outline **one** way in which a business could compete internationally.

....

....

....

....

(2 marks)

3   Explain **one** benefit to a business of using e-commerce to compete internationally.

> E-commerce allows businesses to sell to consumers without needing to open stores.

....

....

....

....

....

....

....

....

....

....

(3 marks)

Ethics and business

The Real Bread Campaign is a UK pressure group that campaigns for producers to declare exactly what goes into bread production, challenges misleading marketing and helps to raise awareness about additives. It campaigns and lobbies for bread that gives nourishment, flavour, digestibility and sustainability.

Source: adapted from www.sustainweb.org

1 State **two** methods that a pressure group such as the Real Bread Campaign could use to influence producers of bread.

    1 ....

    2 .... **(2 marks)**

The Real Bread Campaign could consider two options for a new campaign to encourage manufacturers to make healthier and more sustainable bread products.

Option 1: Publishing a list of manufacturers who produce unhealthy bread

Option 2: Publicly working with a bread producer to produce healthier bread

2 Justify which **one** of these two options the Real Bread Campaign should choose.

> **Guided**

When you answer this question, you could:
- discuss how this action may encourage more manufacturers to change their policies
- discuss the limitations, including how some manufacturers may ignore it or accept the negative publicity
- justify whether or not you believe this is a good decision, and perhaps make recommendations about other ways in which the Real Bread Campaign could influence these businesses or consumers.

Option 1 would help the Real Bread campaign to shame the businesses

on the list into changing their practices ....

....

....

....

....

Option 2 is a more positive strategy ....

....

....

....

....

Overall, I think the Real Bread Campaign should choose ....

....

....

.... **(9 marks)**

Environmental issues

Paperclip is a business that provides office stationery and supplies for business, such as pads, files, binders, paper, storage, equipment and print services. The business has been shortlisted on several green companies award lists for the last three years and recently came first, winning the title of Britain's Best Green Company. This award is given to businesses that successfully focus on their environmental performance and their employees' morale.

1 State **one** method that Paperclip might use to reduce its impact on the environment.

....

.... **(1 mark)**

2 Outline **one** reason why Paperclip might choose to reduce its impact on the environment.

....

....

> Make sure that you relate your answer to Paperclip.

....

....

.... **(2 marks)**

3 Analyse the impact of Paperclip improving its environmentally friendly business practices.

> **Guided**

> When answering this question, you could:
> • consider how its policies will reduce the negative impact on the environment
> • consider how being a green company will also benefit the long-term fortunes of Paperclip.

Improving Paperclip's environmentally friendly business practices will help

the business reduce its carbon footprint. This means that ....

....

....

....

....

....

This might give Paperclip a competitive advantage and ....

....

....

.... **(6 marks)**

Product 1

1 Define the term 'design mix'.

....

.... **(1 mark)**

2 Explain **one** reason why function is an important element of the design mix.

> When answering this question, you could:
> • explain one reason why function is important (for instance, so that the product can do the job that it is intended to do)
> • develop your answer with two linked strands in the form of consequences (for instance, by considering the benefits to a business of selling products that function well).

Guided

Unless a business focuses on function, its product is unlikely to do its

job and therefore meet customer needs ....

....

....

....

.... **(3 marks)**

3 Explain **one** reason why it is important for a business to differentiate its products.

> Differentiation is closely linked to the concepts of competition, adding value and branding.

....

....

....

....

....

....

....

.... **(3 marks)**

Product 2

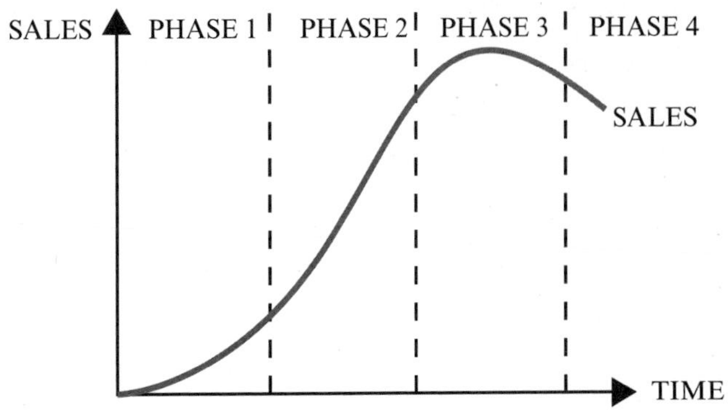

Figure 1 A product life cycle showing sales of a product over a period of time

Guided

1 Look at Figure 1. Which **one** of the following is the name of Phase 4?

Select **one** answer:

☐ **A** Growth

☐ **B** Decline

☐ **C** Maturity

~~☐ **D** Introduction~~

> Introduction is the first phase of the product life cycle, so it can't be Option D.

(1 mark)

2 Define the term 'extension strategy'.

....

.... **(1 mark)**

3 Give **one** possible extension strategy that a business could use.

.... **(1 mark)**

> You do not need to give an explanation when answering a 'give' question.

4 Discuss the benefit to a business of using the product life cycle to make decisions about its products.

....

....

....

....

....

....

....

.... **(6 marks)**

> Look at the product life cycle in Figure 1 and consider how this model could be used to help a business make decisions such as when to launch new products, when to promote products and when to discontinue products.

The importance of price

1   Which **two** of the following actions are **most likely** to help a business increase profits?

Select **two** answers:

☐   **A**   Buy cheaper raw materials used to make its products

☐   **B**   Increase its number of employees

☐   **C**   Increase advertising expenditure

☐   **D**   Increase the sales price of its products

☐   **E**   Buy more expensive raw materials to make its products

(2 marks)

2   Explain **one** reason why a business might increase its prices.

> Think about the impact of a business's total costs on its profit margin.

A business might want to increase its prices if its costs have

increased ....

....

....

....

....

(3 marks)

`Guided`

3   Discuss a reason why price is linked to quality within the marketing mix.

> What pricing strategy might be used when selling a high-quality product?

....

....

....

....

....

....

....

....

....

....

(6 marks)

Had a go ☐ Nearly there ☐ Nailed it! ☐

Pricing strategies

1 Explain **one** way in which technology can influence a business's choice of pricing strategy.

Introducing new technology in the production process can help a

business to reduce its production costs ....

....

....

....

.... **(3 marks)**

> Diva is a clothing retailer in the UK that operates high street retail shops and an e-commerce site. In the period leading up to Christmas 2017, the business's in-store sales fell unexpectedly by 5.6%. On the other hand, its online sales in the same period increased by 3.9%. The business was pleased to find that when it entered its end-of-year sale, it had 5.8% less stock to sell, but sales during the end-of-year sale period were 2% lower than in the previous year.

The following are two strategies that Diva could use in order to maintain its profits when faced with falling sales in stores.

Option 1: Reducing its prices

Option 2: Increasing its advertising

2 Justify which **one** of these two options Diva should choose to maintain its profits.

> When answering this question, you could:
> • consider the impact of increased advertising on customer loyalty, added value, competition and costs
> • consider the impact of reduced prices on customer opinions, competition, total revenue and the contribution per unit
> • consider the effects of both options on Diva's profits, in the short term and in the long term.

....

....

....

....

....

....

....

....

....

....

> For this type of question you must make a judgement about which is the better option. There is no right or wrong answer, but you need to **justify** your choice.

.... **(9 marks)**

Promotion

1   Which **one** of the following is **not** a method of promotion?

Select **one** answer:

☐   **A**   Advertising

☐   **B**   Product trials

☐   **C**   Cutting costs

☐   **D**   Sponsorship   **(1 mark)**

2   Explain **one** reason why a business may use social media to promote its products and services.

> What are the possible benefits of using social media in comparison with other forms of promotion?

....

....

....

....

....

....

....

....   **(3 marks)**

3   Discuss a reason why a business may choose to reduce the amount of promotion that it undertakes.

> Guided

A well-established business may choose to make cutbacks on its

promotion because sales revenue has fallen ....

....

....

....

....

....

....

....

....

....   **(6 marks)**

Had a go ☐   Nearly there ☐   Nailed it! ☐

Promotion, branding and technology

1 Give **two** advantages to a business of having a strong brand.

   1   It gives it the ability to charge a premium price.

   2   .... **(2 marks)**

2 Explain **one** way that a business could use technology to promote itself.

....

....

....

....

....

....

.... **(3 marks)**

> Start by choosing a technology, such as email, websites or social media.

In 2017, the brand valuation business Brand Finance reported that Google became the world's most valuable brand, overtaking Apple. Brand Finance's 2017 report assessed that Apple's brand value fell 36% to just over $107 billion. Meanwhile, the report announced that Google's brand value rose to over $109 billion, up from $88 billion in 2016.

Brand Finance had considered Apple to be the most valuable brand for the previous five years. However, its 2017 report suggested Apple has not retained its technological advantage over its competitors and has faced increasing competition from a number of new smartphone manufacturers.

Source: adapted from Brand Finance *Global 500 2017* report

---

3 Analyse the impact on Google of having the world's most valuable brand.

....

....

....

....

....

....

....

....

.... **(6 marks)**

> When answering this question, you could explain the positive impact of having a brand that is well-known and strong. You could also consider the negative impact of having the most valuable brand in the world. Can you think of any downsides or limitations?

Place

1   Which **two** of the following are **most likely** to be advantages to a retailer of choosing to open a shop on a pedestrianised high street?

> **Guided**

Select **two** answers:

☐   **A**   Availability of customer parking outside the shop

☐   **B**   Suppliers will find it easy to park outside and deliver goods to the shop

☐   **C**   Convenience of location for customers

~~☐   **D**   Locating next to a direct competitor~~

☐   **E**   Potential to attract passing local trade

> The key to a good business location is proximity to customers, resources and trade. Locating next to a direct competitor is unlikely to be an advantage as the rival business may attract some of the retailer's customers.

(2 marks)

2   Explain **one** benefit to a business of using e-commerce to sell its products.

....

....

....

....

....

....

(3 marks)

3   Discuss a factor that a business should consider when choosing a location.

> What is the advantage of trading online in comparison to retail?

....

....

....

....

....

....

....

....

....

....

....

....

(6 marks)

Integrated marketing mix

Samsung is one of the world's largest information technology companies. It is well-regarded and sells products such as computers, televisions, fridge-freezers and smartphones. In 2016, Samsung had to recall its Note 7 smartphone after the business discovered a fault in the battery used in the Note 7. Despite this, its brand value rose 13% between 2016 and 2017.

In 2017, Samsung announced the release of its new range of smartphones, the Galaxy S8 and Galaxy S8+. After Samsung's experience with the Note 7, the business had introduced new and even more rigorous quality and safety testing. Samsung hoped that its new smartphones would restore consumer trust and help its brand to continue competing with other global smartphone brands such as Apple and Huawei.

Source: adapted from http://wccftech.com/galaxy-s8-pre-orders-april-10/

Guided

1 Evaluate the extent to which an integrated marketing mix is the key to the success of the Galaxy S8 and S8+. You should use the information provided and your knowledge of business.

> When answering this question, you could:
> - explain how an integrated marketing mix could help Samsung successfully launch the S8 and S8+ (for instance, how should product and price interact?)
> - explain at least one other factor that Samsung should consider that is not part of the marketing mix (for example, customer service)
> - evaluate the importance of an integrated marketing mix in relation to the other factors you have discussed
> - make recommendations about how Samsung could ensure that the S8 and S8+ succeed.

An integrated marketing mix will help Samsung to market the Galaxy S8 and S8+ effectively to customers at the right price and through the right promotional channels ....

....

....

....

....

....

Overall, an integrated marketing mix is very important and this is especially true for a business who has had negative publicity in the past. Nevertheless, there are ....

....

....

....

....

.... **(12 marks)**

> Will an effective and integrated marketing mix be enough to ensure the success of the new products, or will Samsung need to consider other factors?

Use additional paper to complete your answer.

Business operations and production

1 Give **one** method that a business could use to improve productivity.

....

.... **(1 mark)**

> Remember that explanations are not needed in this type of question.

2 Explain **one** benefit to a business of using batch production.

Guided

One benefit of batch production is that it allows a business to add

variety to its product line ....

....

....

....

....

.... **(3 marks)**

3 Discuss the impact on a business of using flow production.

....

....

....

....

....

> Think about the benefits and downsides of using flow production. Is it suitable for all types of businesses? What impact will it have on costs?

....

....

....

....

....

....

....

....

.... **(6 marks)**

Had a go ☐   Nearly there ☐   Nailed it! ☐

Business operations and technology

Guided

1 Explain **one** way that introducing new technology could improve a business's operations.

> Think of a specific technology. Consider how its introduction might save time, reduce costs or improve the business's productivity.

Introducing new technology could improve a business's operations by

reducing human error ....

....

....

....

.... **(3 marks)**

2 Explain **one** way that a business could use technology to increase its productivity.

> What inputs could a business manage differently?

....

....

....

....

....

.... **(3 marks)**

Guided

3 Discuss a reason why the productivity of a business may fall.

> Productivity is the output of a business divided by its inputs, including time, labour and finance.

As a business's machinery gets older, it becomes less efficient

and might need to be repaired ....

> Productivity can also be linked to the motivation of the workforce.

....

....

....

....

....

....

.... **(6 marks)**

Managing stock

Cara James and Cole Simmons sell models of vehicles, action figures and animals. The models are bought in separate parts from manufacturers and then assembled and painted before sale. Figure 1 shows a bar gate stock graph for their model of a dinosaur.

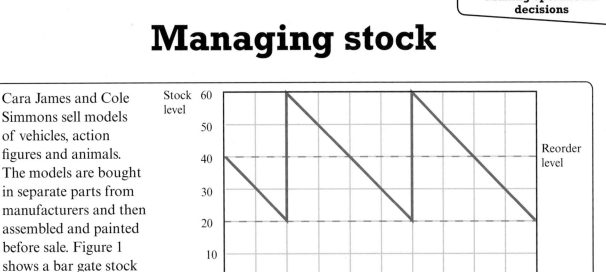

Figure 1

1   Using the graph in Figure 1, identify the number of models that Cara and Cole hold as a buffer stock.

    ....   **(1 mark)**

2   Using the graph in Figure 1, calculate how many weeks it will take for stock of dinosaur models to arrive after the order has been placed. You are advised to show your workings.

> **Guided**

    Stock arrival date – Reorder date
                    = Number of weeks for stock to arrive
                      after reordering

    6 weeks – 4 weeks =

    (2 marks)

3   Explain **one** benefit of just-in-time stock control.

    Why might it be an advantage for a business to hold very little stock?

    ....

    ....

    ....

    ....   **(3 marks)**

Suppliers and procurement

Guided

1   Which **one** of the following is **most likely** to be an impact of a good relationship between a business and its supplier?

Select **one** answer:

☐   **A**   Inflation increases

☐   ~~**B**   The business loses customers~~

☐   **C**   The supplier loses sales

☐   **D**   The business's reputation improves   **(1 mark)**

> A business is likely to lose customers as a result of a **bad** relationship between the business and its suppliers.

2   Explain **one** reason why a business's choice of supplier can affect the success of the business.

....

....

....

....

....

....   **(3 marks)**

3   Discuss the impact of an unprofessional supplier on the competitiveness of a business.

> Think about the impact of logistics on a business's ability to meet the needs of its customers. What might happen if stock didn't arrive on time?

....

....

....

....

....

....

....

....

....

....

....

....

....   **(6 marks)**

Managing quality

1   Explain **one** reason why a business may want to improve the quality of its products.

When a business is known to offer high-quality products and services,

this adds value to its products and services ....

....

....

....   **(3 marks)**

> Werther is a multinational electronics business that makes products such as televisions, cameras, computers and home appliances. In 2017, the business launched a 60-inch television that incorporated new technologies such as ultra-high definition (UHD) and 4k screen resolution.

Werther is considering two different options that it could use to ensure that the new television and its other products are of the highest possible quality.

Option 1: Introduce quality control

Option 2: Introduce quality assurance

2   Justify which **one** of these options Werther should choose.

> When answering this question, you might want to consider:
> • the cost of quality control and the problems of checking at the end of the production process
> • the cost of implementing a culture of quality assurance within a business
> • the impact of quality assurance on staff and regulation
> • the type of business and whether the benefits outweigh the costs over time.

....

....

....

....

....

....

....

....

....

> You must make a well-supported judgement about which option you think is better. Make sure that your answer focuses specifically on the business in the case study and is justified.

....

....

....   **(9 marks)**

Customer service and the sales process

1 Which **one** of the following is **most likely** to improve a business's customer service?

Select **one** answer

☐ **A**   Setting sales objectives

☐ **B**   Limiting the range of products that it sells

☐ **C**   Providing guaranteed on-time delivery to customers

☐ **D**   Launching a new advertising campaign   **(1 mark)**

2 Give **two** stages of the sales process.

> What is the next stage after customer engagement, once the customer has bought the product?

1   Customer engagement

> **Guided**

2   ....   **(2 marks)**

RightOnTime Cabs is a taxi business in the north-east of England. It prides itself on never being more than 2 minutes late to pick up any passengers and it specialises in taking customers to airports in Durham and Newcastle. There are eight other taxi firms within 10 miles of its location and it recognises the need for effective customer service.

RightOnTime Cabs is considering two options to improve customer service and give the business a competitive advantage.

Option 1: Guaranteeing that a RightOnTime cab will never be more than 5 minutes late

Option 2: Giving a 10% discount on a customer's second booking

3 Justify which **one** of these options RightOnTime Cabs should choose.

> When answering this question, you have to decide which option you think will improve customer service and provide RightOnTime Cabs with a competitive advantage. Make sure that your answer focuses specifically on the business in the case study and is justified.

....

....

....

....

....

....

....

....   **(9 marks)**

Gross and net profit

1 Which **one** of the following is **most likely** to lead to an increase in a business's profits in the short term?

Select **one** answer:

☐ **A** Electricity prices remaining the same

☐ **B** An increase in the number of sales

☐ **C** A rise in costs

☐ **D** Employing more people **(1 mark)**

2 Define the term 'gross profit'.

....

.... **(1 mark)**

3 Using the information below calculate the net profit for the business. You are advised to show your workings.

> Guided

Gross profit: £200

Other operating costs: £115

Net profit = Gross profit − Other operating costs

Net profit = £200 − £115

> It may help you to write out the formula first, then highlight the relevant information in the accounts.

£..

(2 marks)

Had a go ☐   **Nearly there** ☐   **Nailed it!** ☐

Profit margins and ARR

Table 1 is the income statement for Performance Sports Ltd.

Sales revenue	
Personal training sessions	£17 000
Team training sessions	£13 000
Total sales	**£30 000**
Costs	
Cost of sales	£7000
Gross profit	**£23 000**
Other costs	£8250
Net profit	**£14 750**

Table 1

Guided

1   Using the information in Table 1, calculate the net profit margin for Performance Sports Ltd. You are advised to show your workings.

$$\text{Net profit margin (\%)} = \frac{\text{Net profit}}{\text{Sales revenue}} \times 100$$

$$\text{Net profit margin} = \frac{£14\,750}{£30\,000} \times 100$$

....%

(2 marks)

Performance Sports Ltd is planning to undertake a project requiring an initial investment of £400 000. Table 2 shows the expected profits of the project.

Year	Year 1	Year 2	Year 3	Year 4	Year 5
Profit	£100 000	£200 000	£180 000	£120 000	£100 000

Table 2

2   Using the information in Table 2, calculate the average rate of return of the project. You are advised to show your workings.

> You may find it helpful to write out the formula for average rate of return before you start your calculations. Remember to show your workings.

....%

(2 marks)

Interpreting quantitative business data

What do consumers want most from wearable technology?

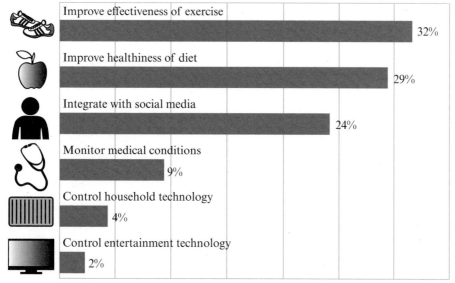

Figure 1

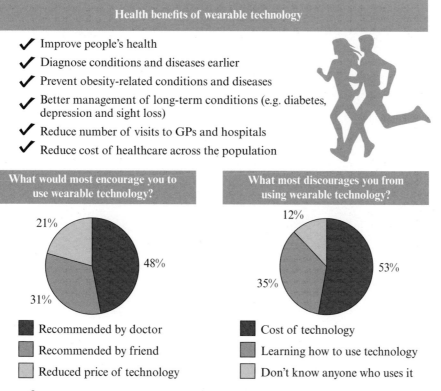

Figure 2

Figure 1 shows the results of a customer survey into consumers' expectations of wearable technology.

1 Identify **one** feature that consumers would like from wearable technology.

....

.... **(1 mark)**

Questions continue on the next page.

Had a go ☐   Nearly there ☐   Nailed it! ☐

Limitations of quantitative data

Figure 2 shows the results of a consumer survey into attitudes towards wearable technology.

2   Identify the **most likely** reason that would encourage people to adopt wearable technology.

....   **(1 mark)**

3   Using the information in Figure 2, analyse the impact of improvements to wearable technology on healthcare providers.

> **Guided**

> Identify one or two key pieces of information from Figure 2. Relate this information to healthcare businesses and how these improvements to wearable technology may create opportunities or threats for these businesses.

Wearable technology such as smart watches is a technology that will

support the healthcare industry by reducing costs ....

....

....

....

....

....

....

....

....   **(6 marks)**

4   Discuss a reason why a business may use **both** qualitative data **and** quantitative data when making business decisions.

....

....

....

....

....

....

....

....

....

> Remember that qualitative data is based on attitudes, reasons and opinions, whereas quantitative data is based on numbers and statistics.

....   **(6 marks)**

Organisational structures

1   Which **one** of the following is a benefit of a flat business structure?

Select **one** answer:

☐   **A**   The business has very clear lines of authority

☐   **B**   There are plenty of opportunities for promotion within the business

☐   **C**   The business can be more flexible

☐   **D**   The business is very easy to control   **(1 mark)**

2   Define the term 'hierarchical structure'.

....

.... **(1 mark)**

3   Give **one** reason why a business might adopt a decentralised structure.

....

....

.... **(1 mark)**

> Remember that
> you do not need to
> explain your answer
> to a 'give' question.

4   Discuss the impact on a business of centralised decision-making.

> **Guided**

When answering this question, you may want to consider the effects of centralised
decision-making on:
• the kind of decisions that are made
• control over business activities
• employees.

A benefit of centralising decisions is that the business will be able to

ensure that all of the decisions are being made in line with company

policy ....

....

....

....

....

....

....

....

....

....

.... **(6 marks)**

Had a go ☐   Nearly there ☐   Nailed it! ☐

The importance of effective communication

The Colquit family started its first bakery over 40 years ago. It has recently expanded and now has over 30 stores in villages and small towns in the south-west. The CrustCake Bakery is keen to ensure that the same high standard is maintained in all its shops. With expansion and the need for more workers, the business experienced communication problems. Sometimes changes to ingredients were not sent to all shops and quality fell. At other times, there was too much information, instructions were ignored and deliveries were late. Customers started to shop at other places.

1   State **one** barrier to effective communication in the CrustCake Bakery.

   ....

   .... **(1 mark)**

2   Evaluate whether the CrustCake Bakery would benefit from improving communication within the business. You should use the information provided as well as your knowledge of business.

Guided

   When answering this question, you may want to:
   • consider the advantages of good communication to the CrustCake Bakery
   • consider whether a goal to improve communication is more important, as important or less important than other goals, such as improving cash flow or lowering prices
   • explain which benefit of good communication would be most significant for the CrustCake Bakery
   • make a justified judgement about the importance of clear communication to the CrustCake Bakery.

   Communication is especially important for a business such as the

   CrustCake Bakery, which has 30 small bakeries across the south-west

   region. This is because ....

   ....

   ....

   ....

   Although communication is important, other factors are also significant.

   Having a large number of small bakeries will be very expensive to run, so

   ....

   ....

   Overall, communication is very important because ....

   ....

   Nevertheless, improving communication will be pointless if ....

   ....

   .... **(12 marks)**

Use additional paper to complete your answer.

Different ways of working

1   Explain **one** benefit to a business of part-time employees.

....

....

....

....

....

.... **(3 marks)**

2   Explain **one** reason why a business might use freelance contract employees.

> Freelance contract employees are not permanent employees and
>
> may be brought in to complete a certain function for a business

> Freelance contract employees might have a specialist skill or experience.

Guided

....

....

....

.... **(3 marks)**

3   Discuss a way in which technology could improve the way that people work in a business.

> When answering this question, you may want to:
> - identify a specific technology and explain how employees use it for work
> - explain how this technology improves aspects of the business, such as its flexibility, its communication and the amount of time that it saves.

....

....

....

....

....

....

....

....

....

....

.... **(6 marks)**

Different job roles and responsibilities

1 Which **one** of the following documents is **not likely** to be used in the recruitment process when hiring a new employee?

> Guided

Select **one** answer:

☐ ~~A Job description~~

☐ **B** Business plan

☐ **C** Application form

☐ **D** Job advertisement

> It isn't Option A because job descriptions are used in the recruitment process.

(1 mark)

> Colin Murphy runs a small travel agency. He has three shops and employs ten people. Colin now wants to hire someone with knowledge of adventure holidays as he thinks this is likely to be a growth area.

2 State **two** job roles that may exist within Colin Murphy's business.

> Think about the different roles that a travel agency like Colin Murphy's might need. Who sells the business's holidays to customers?

1 ....

2 .... **(2 marks)**

3 Explain **one** responsibility of a manager in a business.

....

....

....

....

....

.... **(3 marks)**

Effective recruitment

1 Explain **one** reason why a business would request references as part of the recruitment process.

....

....

....

....

....

(3 marks)

> The details of referees may be included on a person's CV.

2 Explain **one** reason why a manager may draw up a person specification for a new role within the business.

....

....

....

....

(3 marks)

> A person specification is not the same as a job description or a CV.

Read about Colin Murphy on page 80.

3 Analyse the impact on Colin Murphy's travel agency of using external recruitment to fill the vacancy.

Guided

> When answering this question, you may want to consider:
> • the benefits of external recruitment for a small business
> • the downsides of external recruitment for a small business
> • how these factors affect the choice of recruitment type.
>
> Make sure that your answer focuses specifically on Colin Murphy's business.

Using external recruitment will allow Colin to increase his workforce

and bring a new person into the business who is ....

....

....

....

External recruitment can be costly and it takes time for new employees

to settle into the business before they are fully productive and

integrated ....

....

....

....

(6 marks)

Developing employees

1   Explain **one** benefit to a business of the use of employee target setting and performance reviews.

Performance management helps businesses to achieve their aims. This

is because ....

....

....

....

....

....
          (3 marks)

> Philip Wragg runs AutoSure, a car mechanics business that provides a range of services including paintwork repair, bodywork, MOTs, and engine repair. He is looking to expand the range of services his business offers to include upgrades and maintenance of car on-board computers. Philip employs six mechanics and is considering sending them all on a formal training course to improve their skills.

Philip is considering two options to develop his employees' skills.

Option 1: Send all employees on a formal training course

Option 2: Implement a coaching system where senior employees train junior employees

2   Justify which **one** of these two options Philip should choose.

> When answering this question, you could:
> - analyse the benefits and drawbacks of Option 1
> - analyse the benefits and drawbacks of Option 2
> - decide which option you think is best and justify your decision
> - suggest ways in which Philip could effectively manage the training of his workers.

....

....

....

....

....

....

....

....

....

> What might be the limitations of some mechanics informally training other mechanics?

....   **(9 marks)**

Use additional paper to complete your answer.

The importance of training

1 Explain **one** reason why a business might encourage its employees to engage in self-learning.

....

....

....

....

....

....   **(3 marks)**

2 Explain **one** benefit to a business of investing in employee training.

> When answering this question, you could consider the impact on employees' skills or the impact on employee motivation and retention.

One benefit of investing in training is that it can help improve

motivation in the workforce ....

....

....

....

....   **(3 marks)**

3 Discuss the impact of training employees to use new technology.

> When answering this question, you could:
> • discuss how new technology can help to improve productivity in the long term
> • discuss the short-term impact on productivity of adopting new technology.

....

....

....

....

....

....

....

....

....   **(6 marks)**

Motivating employees 1

1 Which **one** of the following best describes the term 'commission'?

Select **one** answer:

☐ **A** An annual payment paid in equal instalments

☐ **B** A percentage of the value of a sale paid to the salesperson

☐ **C** A one-off bonus for long service with the business

☐ **D** A payment for every hour worked

(1 mark)

> Option C is a definition of a bonus payment, so it can't be a definition of commission.

2 Give **one** financial method that a business could use to motivate employees.

....

....

(1 mark)

3 Explain **one** disadvantage to a business of paying employees by the hour.

....

....

....

....

....

....

(3 marks)

> Link your answer to how the remuneration method will motivate employees.

4 Discuss the impact on a business of paying its staff using a bonus scheme.

> When answering this question, you could consider:
> • how staff would react to the introduction of a bonus scheme
> • how the business will be affected by the introduction of a bonus scheme.

....

....

....

....

....

....

....

....

....

....

(6 marks)

Motivating employees 2

Carltens is a small chain of cafes in the Midlands. The business is facing competition from coffee shops such as Starbucks, Costa and Caffè Nero. The business has decided to look at ways to improve staff motivation.

1 State **one** reason why staff motivation is important to Carltens.

....

.... **(1 mark)**

2 Outline **one** method that Carltens could use to improve staff motivation.

Carltens could introduce job enrichment by giving employees the

opportunity to ....

....

....

.... **(2 marks)**

Carltens is considering introducing an employee reward scheme to recognise high-performing employees.

3 Analyse the impact on Carltens of introducing the employee reward scheme.

When answering this question, you could:
- explain how the scheme will boost employee motivation
- discuss the impact on the business's performance of having more motivated employees
- explain the drawbacks of the scheme in relation to other approaches to motivation.

....

....

....

....

....

....

....

....

....

Consider the impact on employees who don't receive the reward. How might they feel?

....

....

.... **(6 marks)**

Exam skills: Case study

Answer ALL questions.
Look at Figures 1 and 2 and read the following extract carefully, then answer the questions.
Write your answers in the spaces provided.

Jaguar is Britain's biggest car maker and is owned by the Indian multinational, Tata Motors. The business employs nearly 40 000 people in the UK (report dated June 2017). In 2018, Jaguar will launch its new electric sport car, the I-Pace, which can accelerate to 60 mph in around 4 seconds and is part of Jaguar's strategy to compete in the electric car market. The I-Pace can travel around 300 miles on a single charge and will be manufactured in Austria.

Other models in Jaguar's range, such as the XF and XE, have won prestigious industry awards such as Most Reliable Family Car and Executive Car of the Year. Between October and December 2016, Jaguar's sales revenues grew by 13% to £65.5 bn. However, in the same period, the company's net profit fell to £255 m, which was a decrease of 49% on the previous year's results.

Figure 1

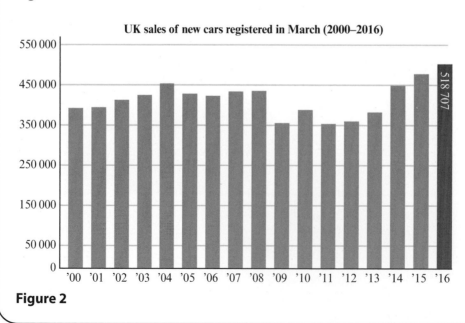

Figure 2

Had a go ☐   Nearly there ☐   Nailed it! ☐

Exam skills: Practice paper

1 Using the information in Figure 2, identify a trend in sales of new cars.

> A trend is the general direction in which a statistic changes (for instance, up or down) over a particular period. Look at the period between 2011 and 2016 and identify the trend.

....

....

(1 mark)

2 Outline **one** reason why Jaguar might produce its cars in another country.

Guided

> How might manufacturing in a different country affect the business's costs or its access to skilled labour?

If the car manufacturing industry is well-established in Austria, Jaguar

may choose to manufacture its cars there because..............................

....

....

....

(2 marks)

3 Calculate Jaguar's net profit margin in 2016 between the period October to December. You are advised to show your workings.

> Give your answer to two decimal places. You may also find it helpful to write down the formula before you start your calculation.

....%

(2 marks)

Had a go ☐   **Nearly there** ☐   **Nailed it!** ☐

4   Analyse the impact on Jaguar's organisational structure of the size of its workforce.

> When answering this question, you could:
> - analyse how Jaguar might divide up its workforce (e.g. into functions and departments across different divisions and different countries)
> - analyse the type of structure that would suit Jaguar and allow it to manage 40 000 employees.

....

....

....

....

....

....

....

....

....

....

....

....

....

....

....

.... **(6 marks)**

5 Analyse the benefit to Jaguar of receiving industry awards.

Guided

> Consider the effect of industry awards on customers' opinions about the Jaguar brand. How could Jaguar use these awards in its promotion activities?

Receiving industry awards such as Best Executive Car will help Jaguar

to attract lots of positive free publicity. This helps the business to

....

....

....

....

....

Another benefit is the internal impact that receiving awards will have

on the business's engineers, designers and sales staff...........................

....

....

....

....

....

....

....   **(6 marks)**

Jaguar could consider two options to improve sales of its electric car in the UK.

Option 1: Increase promotion of the new product

Option 2: Run limited product trials in different areas of the UK

6   Justify which **one** of these options Jaguar should choose.

> A 'justify' question requires you to consider the benefits and drawbacks of two options, then choose one option and support your choice using evidence from the case study and your own knowledge of business. Your answer to this question must be rooted in the context of Jaguar and the car industry.

....

....

....

....

....

....

....

....

....

....

....

....

....

....

....

....

....

....

....

.... **(9 marks)**

Jaguar is a prestigious car brand and is well-known for producing luxury sports cars such as the Jaguar F-Type.

> Guided

7 Evaluate whether Jaguar's choice to compete in the electric car market is a good decision for the business. You should use the information provided as well as your knowledge of business.

> When answering this question:
> - ensure that your answer is in context of Jaguar and the car industry
> - explain the benefits to Jaguar of entering the electric car market
> - explain the risks to Jaguar of entering the electric car market and competing with companies that are already established in the industry
> - consider the importance of selling cars that are environmentally friendly
> - come to a balanced decision about whether it is a good or bad idea for Jaguar to compete in the electric car market, including clear justification and recommendations to Jaguar.

Entering the electric car market will bring Jaguar a number of benefits.

The first is that consumers are becoming more environmentally

conscious so ....

....

....

....

....

....

> What factors might affect Jaguar's success of competing in the electric car market?

However, Jaguar is better known for its high-powered luxury sports

cars like the F-Type, and ....

....

....

....

....

....

Overall, it is a good idea for Jaguar to enter the electric car market

at this point. Figure 2 shows ....

....

....

.... **(12 marks)**

Use additional paper to complete your answer.

Answers

Theme 1: Investigating small business

The following pages contain suggested answers to the questions in Theme 1 of the Revision Workbook. In many cases, these are not the only correct answers.

1. The dynamic nature of business

1   D
2   Changing consumer needs creates a gap in the market. If the business can satisfy these needs, it will be able to charge customers a premium price, which allows the business to generate a greater profit margin.
3   An advantage of developing a new idea from an existing product or service is that the business owner knows the basic idea is already successful. Developing an existing idea is therefore less high risk than launching a brand new idea, as it allows a business owner to expand an existing and successful product or service to meet the needs of more consumers.
4   One factor that an entrepreneur may consider before opening a new business is whether or not there is a consumer need for the products that the business will offer. Up-to-date market research allows an entrepreneur to spot unfulfilled consumer needs and identify potential gaps in the market. If there is insufficient demand for the product offered by a new business, it is likely that the business will fail due to a lack of revenue. Considering consumer needs also allows an entrepreneur to estimate potential demand and how much of a product they should manufacture for the business launch, so that they are not surprised by their product being very popular and running out of stock.

2. Risk and reward

1   A
2   Running a business can involve high levels of risk because demand can quickly change. This means that a business's sales might fall very suddenly due to an increase in competition. This could lead to a business losing revenue, failing to make a profit and having to close down.
3   A business owner could reduce the risk of their business by carrying out market research. Market research will allow an owner to understand the market and make appropriate decisions to run the business well. It also enables the owner to anticipate customer demand, allowing them to ensure that the business holds the correct amount of stock to meet customers' needs. Another way that a business owner could reduce risk is through effective planning. Creating a detailed business plan makes the business owner consider all the issues associated with running their business and means that they are more likely to have anticipated potential problems.

3. The role of business enterprise

1   A
2   D
3   A business can meet the needs of its customers by providing high-quality products. If products are high quality, they are less likely to break or be faulty. This means that customers will be satisfied and will feel as though they have received value for their money.

4. The importance of added value

1   The sale of exotic flowers.
2   The Witney Flower Shop could add value to its products by offering its customers a delivery service. This will make it more convenient for some customers to buy flowers.
3   Being located on a high street means the business is more visible to passing trade. This adds value because customers may recognise the brand because they have seen it on the high street and may feel that they are buying flowers from a well-established business. This means that Ellie may be seen as trustworthy and her flowers as more prestigious. Furthermore, being located on a high street makes it easier for customers to visit the shop when buying from other local businesses. This adds value because the shop is more convenient and customers may be willing to pay a high price for products that are more accessible and therefore save them time when shopping.

5. The role of entrepreneurship

1   C
2   A and C
3   Entrepreneurs benefit the economy because they create jobs. This is because successful new businesses normally grow, which means they need more employees to work for them. These new jobs reduce the level of unemployment in the economy. Entrepreneurs also create products and services that people want and desire. When consumers go out and buy these new products and services, they spend money, which boosts economic activity and growth. This can also lead to additional tax revenue for the government as people pay VAT on an increased number of purchases.

6. Customer needs 1

1   46%
2   27%
3   Customer service is important because it is linked to the experience a customer has when they buy a product. If customer service is good, it is more likely that customers will be satisfied with their experience. This means that they are more likely to return to the business and become a repeat customer.

7. Customer needs 2

1   Option 1 may encourage customers to use Samit's service instead of booking another service such as a local taxi company. Furthermore, customers may also book and pay in advance for a number of trips, and this would help to improve his cash flow.
    Offering to pick up customers over 60 may also be a good option, as this segment of his market may value convenience more than other segments of the market. Picking customers up from their homes would certainly provide a more convenient service. However, other customers may not be happy with this as it may lengthen their journey time to the airport. In addition, only 9% of the people who responded to his market research fell into this market segment, so there may not be a significant number of people who are looking for this type of service.
    Overall, I believe that Samit should offer customers Option 2. Although fewer people are likely to want this service, because it is limited to the segment of his market aged 60 or over, he could start to open this option up to other customers. This would make his service very convenient and allow him to compete with taxi companies who might provide this service at a premium.

8. The role of market research

1   Possible answers include:
    • the least important factor to customers is the shop's layout
    • opening hours are a less important factor than the friendliness of staff
    • the most important factor to customers is whether the shop's products meet their needs
    • value for money is a more important factor than the friendliness of staff.

2 Conduct and read surveys about customers' buying habits when purchasing clothing, which will allow the business to see what styles or items of clothing customers are interested in purchasing.

3 Market research can help a business to decide the price at which it should sell its products. The business would be able to compare competitors offering similar products in order to identify the best price range that it could charge for its own products. This might allow it to offer competitive prices that would encourage more customers to buy from the business rather than from its rivals.

9. Types of market research

1 Possible answers include:
- questionnaire
- survey
- focus group
- observation.

2 Primary market research is collected first-hand so it is likely to be more reliable: a business is more likely to be able to trust the data that it has gathered for itself because this data is tailored to its needs. As a result, the business can have more confidence in the business decisions that it makes using this information.

3 Secondary market research can be quick and easy to get hold of because it has already been collected by a third party and is often available on the internet through sources such as government agencies. This may be appealing to a business because it will take far less time and less money to collect than most forms of primary research. Another advantage of secondary research over primary research is that primary research normally involves a small sample size. A small sample size means that the business cannot be as confident that the data is representative of the whole population or its customer base. This means that data based on a larger sample size is likely to be more reliable; enabling the business to make well-justified decisions.

10. Market research data

1 100 customers.

2 Market research data might be biased because the people involved may already know the business owner (such as friends of the business owner). This might mean that they are more likely to give positive responses to a questionnaire because they want to be nice. As a result, the results of the questionnaire will not be a true reflection of what most consumers think.

3 The limitations of the research carried out by the clothing company are that it is only a sample of 100 people and the results are quantitative. Quantitative data is good if the owners want to calculate statistics, but it does not give the reasons behind customers' responses, such as why 11 customers liked the late opening hours or how the business provides value for money. A focus group would allow customers to discuss their ideas, share opinions and give far more detailed responses. The owners could observe these discussions and record the answers. This would provide qualitative data, which may be far more useful in helping the owners to make decisions. For example, if they better understand what their customers want, they could increase the number of customers who feel that the shop sells the clothes that they want. Similarly, qualitative research data could help them to understand what makes their staff friendly and to improve customer service. The business may find that qualitative market research data takes longer and costs more to gather, but it may help the business to make better long-term business decisions.

11. Market segmentation

1 Possible answers include:
- by age
- by gender
- by income
- by location
- by lifestyle
- by demographics.

2 One limitation of market segmentation is that focusing on one segment can cause a business to miss another opportunity elsewhere. This is because other market segments could be far more profitable. As a result, focusing on one segment could lead to an opportunity cost for a business.

3 Focusing on a specific market segment makes it easier for a business to develop products and services. This is because it can focus the features and functions of its products and services to meet the specific needs of its chosen market segment. This can result in products being more desirable and the business being better able to meet customer needs. Another benefit is that market research becomes far easier when dealing with specific market segments. This is because there is a smaller potential population size and it will be easier for a business to gather a representative sample size. As a result, its business decisions will be more accurate.

12. Market mapping

1 One benefit of Option 1 is that there is a gap in the market in his local town for restaurants offering South American cuisine. This means that there are no other restaurants of this type, so Mario's business would be unlikely to face any direct competition. However, this does not necessarily mean that the business will be a success. There is no research available on local customers' preferences, so Mario does not know whether there is a gap in the market because there is no demand for this cuisine in Odmoor.

On the other hand, there are four restaurants offering British cuisine, suggesting that Option 2 might be popular with local consumers. In addition, there is a number of cheaper restaurants in the area and this might be because consumers in the local area prefer cheaper prices to premium prices, again suggesting that Option 2 could be more popular. However, the disadvantage of Option 2 is that there are already restaurants offering medium-priced British cuisine, meaning that Mario's business would be more likely to face direct competition. Overall, I think Mario should choose Option 1. Entrepreneurs need to take risks and if his restaurant is popular then there is every chance of it being a success because of the lack of direct competition. Its success will also depend on the quality and reputation of Toni's Bistro (the closest competitor) and also on the level of demand for this cuisine. As a result, Mario should carry out further research into local consumers' preferences and the other local restaurants in the area before making his final decision.

13. Competition

1 Market research showing that there was demand for farm-produced dairy ice cream.

2 The Trembaths offer ice cream in any flavour ordered by customers. This differentiates their ice cream from others because other manufacturers cannot do this.

3 Valerie and Norman could differentiate their ice cream by using a unique logo and packaging that emphasises the local Cornish nature of their brand. This will help the Trembaths to build a solid Cornish brand that may be more likely to be stocked in local shops, cafés and restaurants.

14. Competitive markets

1 If a large number of businesses sell a very similar type of product, this could force many of those businesses to compete on price as they are unable to differentiate their product from their competitors' in any other way. This might lead to lower profit margins for those businesses.

2 A new competitor entering the market could lead to a number of hotels and restaurants choosing to stock the new ice cream instead of Truro's Best. This would be especially true if the new competitor's product was offered to restaurants at a cheaper price, considering that Truro's Best is a premium-priced product. However, Truro's Best is a local ice cream and many local businesses may prefer to stock a product that is local and therefore benefits the local community and attracts a higher price from their customers. This may mean that Valerie and Norman will be able to cope with a new competitor entering the local ice cream market.

15. Aims and objectives

1 Independence (wanting to be her own boss).

2 Possible answers include:
- supporting charities that promote outdoor activities for disadvantaged young people
- opening a second shop in order to challenge the business.

3 An objective to break-even could be set because the business might be a newly established start-up, so this is an appropriate target for a new business. By breaking even, the business will cover its costs and this means that the owner will not be in any debt and the business will not be making a loss.

16. Differing aims and objectives

1 Anna's business has achieved the main aim that she set for its first two years of trading, because it has survived and is still trading. The business has not failed within this time, as many businesses do, which suggests that the business is and has the potential to be successful. The fact that Anna has started to make a profit means that her business could continue to grow, so she is right to set an ambitious new aim. Figure 1 also suggests that a large proportion of her customers come from elsewhere in Scotland, so a second shop closer to these customers may solidify and increase the business's customer base in those areas.

On the other hand, the business has not yet repaid its start-up costs, so Anna might want to set a new aim of repaying her debt instead. If Anna does not repay the debt that she owes her father, this might cause a breakdown in their relationship. Repaying the start-up costs might also mean that the business finds it easier to borrow money from other sources in order to fund its expansion plans.

Opening a second shop might also be ambitious because the business is only just starting to make a profit. If the business grows too quickly, it could face diseconomies of scale, which could cause it to lose money, or it could experience cash flow problems, which could cause it to fail. However, the business is in a strong cash-flow position, which suggests that expansion could be a viable option.

Overall, I believe that setting a new aim of expanding the business by opening a second shop is a reasonable objective for Anna's business. As businesses become established, it is good for the owners to set ambitious aims and objectives, and growing the business at a steady rate will make it safer in the long term. The success of the business may depend on the demand in the market and how well her products and customer service are differentiated from those of competitors. In order for Anna to achieve this aim, she must make sure she has an accurate cash-flow forecast and understands the market to ensure there is sufficient demand for a second shop.

17. Revenues and costs

1 £1200

2 £2400

3 Reducing the variable cost per unit would mean each item sold has a greater profit margin. As a result, it will take the business less time to break even and its chances of making a profit would increase.

18. Profit and loss

1 Possible answers include:
- buy cheaper raw materials used to make its ceramic plates
- increase the sales price of an average plate
- relocate to cheaper premises.

2 Possible answers include:
- sales of plates may have fallen, causing a fall in revenue
- the business may have cut prices but sales of plates did not rise, causing a fall in revenue.

3 Loan = £5000
Total repayments = 48 × £116.50 = £5592
Interest = £5592 − £5000 = £592

Total interest = $\frac{£592}{£5000} \times 100 = 11.84\%$

4 (i) £2200, (ii) £200, (iii) £2100, (iv) £2700

19. Break-even charts

1 D

2 16

3 £10000

4 £2000

20. Using break-even

1 Reduce the fixed costs of running the recording studio.

2 13 sessions (rounded up from 12.5 sessions).
Break-even = Total fixed costs ÷ (Price − Variable cost per item)
Break-even = 4000 ÷ (570 − 250)
= 4000 ÷ 320
= 12.5

3 Break-even analysis is a useful tool to help Yffects make business decisions because the business only sells one service. If the business is able to accurately estimate its fixed and variable costs then it can use break-even analysis to work out exactly how many recording sessions it needs to sell in order to cover its costs. Break-even analysis can also help Yffects answer 'what if?' questions, such as 'what would happen if we increase prices?' or 'what would happen if we reduced variable costs?' The limitation of break-even analysis is that it does not help the business estimate the number of bookings that it will receive.

21. Calculating cash-flow

1 −£4000

2 £14000

3 (i) −£7000, (ii) £14000, (iii) −£11000

22. The importance of cash to a business

1 D

2 A strong cash flow is important to a business because cash helps a business to expand. If a business has plenty of cash, it can afford to invest in growth. In the long term, this will help a business to increase its profits.

3 Delaying payments would help to maintain a positive net cash flow because it would help counteract the late payments that the business receives from customers. However, delaying payment could affect Jayston Printing's reputation because suppliers will be unhappy that payment is delayed. As a result, some suppliers may choose not to work with Jayston Printing and this could reduce the number of suppliers willing to work with the business. This in turn could lead to higher variable costs, as the business has less choice about which suppliers it can work with.

23. Short-term sources of finance

1 Possible answers include:
   - arrange an overdraft
   - negotiate better trade credit arrangements with suppliers
   - request faster payment from customers.
2 Gurrinder could arrange an overdraft with her bank. This would help her cover the upfront costs of the new website and the increase in advertising without having to take out a loan.
3 A business could use trade credit. This would allow the business to pay its suppliers at a later date, once it has received revenue from sales. This helps the business to improve its cash-flow position by deferring cash outflow until it has received cash inflow.

24. Long-term sources of finance

1 Gurrinder could use a bank loan to finance her expansion into designing shops, factories and film sets. A bank loan is a long-term source of finance that will need to be repaid with interest.
2 Retained profit is a good long-term source of finance because it does not need to be repaid. This means that choosing Option 1 would ensure that Gurrinder does not accrue any debt to pay for her new shop designs and set designs. However, it is likely that the expansion of her business will require a large amount of investment. It is unlikely that, as a sole trader operating a small business, Gurrinder will have made enough profit that she could have retained in order to pay for everything she needs to grow her business.
   Option 2 may be a suitable option as crowd funding is often used by small creative businesses that can struggle to attract one or two large-scale private investors. Crowd funding might also be a useful option because it would allow Gurrinder to promote her business through a crowd funding website and raise awareness of her brand. It could also help her to attract capital from a large number of potential investors without having to give them much or any control over her business, rather than having to seek out one or two private investors who are more likely to want to have some control over the business's decisions.
   Overall, I believe that Option 2 would be the better option for Gurrinder to take because it is more likely to raise enough money to fund the expansion of Be Different than Option 1. In addition, there is relatively little risk associated with Option 2 if Gurrinder is not able to raise the amount of money she has targeted. However, this depends on exactly how much capital she believes she will need to raise in order to fund the expansion of Be Different and how well she can promote her idea to potential crowd-funding investors.

25. Limited liability

1 D
2 C and D
3 One benefit of changing a business into a private limited company is that the business owner will now have limited liability. This means that they can only lose the sum of the capital that they invested into the business and their personal assets are protected. The business owner may also be one of several shareholders, and this means that they can share the responsibility of running the business with the other shareholders. This might help to spread the workload and bring new ideas and skills into the business.

26. Types of business ownership

1 A private limited company is a business that has limited liability and is owned by shareholders.
2 Possible answers include:
   - having sole responsibility for running the business
   - having unlimited liability.
3 A private limited company can sell shares to other people known to the owner of the business. These people become shareholders, and this process allows the business to raise more capital than if it was a sole trader.

4 Limited businesses are often larger and more established businesses. Private limited businesses are also registered with Companies House, meaning that customers are able to track down the owners and registered business premises if anything goes wrong with their transaction. Another reason why customers may trust private limited businesses more is that a private limited company has a separate bank account to its owners and is treated as a separate legal entity from its owners by the legal system. This can sometimes mean that it is easier for customers to get their money back if anything goes wrong.

27. Franchising

1 Sandie will be able to get guidance and advice about running a pet care business and providing grooming services from Happy Dog.
2 If Sandie opens a Happy Dog franchise she will receive lots of support in how to set up and run her new business. Equipment and services such as dog grooming equipment, uniforms and advertising will also be provided by the franchisor. This could be especially useful for Sandie because she has never run her own business and will lack essential business experience that the franchisor can provide.
   However, £9995 is a lot of money to invest in a new business and Sandie may have to borrow this money from a bank or family member. Furthermore, Happy Dog will take a percentage of her business's sales revenue, which means that she will need to generate considerable revenue in order to pay off fixed costs (potentially including an initial loan to pay for the franchise).
   Overall, I believe that it is better for Sandie to take out the franchise than to start her own business. Even though she has a love of animals, this does not guarantee that she knows how to run a successful business and opening an established franchise will reduce the risk of failure.

28. Business location

1 Possible answers include:
   - proximity to competitors
   - proximity to labour market
   - access to transport links.
2 The business will be noticed by lots of potential customers. This means that there is more chance of customers entering the business's premises to purchase goods and services than if the business was located on a side street out of view. This could lead to higher sales revenues.
3 An exporter may choose a location that has easy access to ports or airports, depending on the nature of the products it sells. This location would make it easier for the business to transport its goods abroad to its target market. This would also reduce the business's transport costs. An exporter may also want to be located in a location where rent and business rates are low. This is because its main customers are abroad. Occupying a prime UK retail location will therefore be less important to the business than if it sold products to UK customers, because this means that it does not need to be in close proximity to customers in order to attract sales. Instead, the business can pass on the savings that it gains from lower costs to its customers by selling its products at a lower price; thus gaining a competitive advantage.

29. The marketing mix

1 C
2 D
3 The price element of the marketing mix could be used to promote the fact that Goalz intends to sell its app on the Apple App Store at a lower price than competitors' apps.

30. Influences on the marketing mix

1 Technology could influence the marketing mix by lowering the prices of a business's products. This is because new technology can make manufacturing products less expensive. This allows the business to charge its customers a lower price, which makes its products more competitive in the market.

2 Because Amy targets a specific segment of the party organising market (that found in and around Cheltenham), it is important that she reaches potential customers in the local area. This will influence the specific promotion methods that she decides to use, such as advertising in local magazines and sponsoring local businesses. Using these promotion methods could increase Amy's total costs considerably and she will have to take this into account when setting the prices for her party organising services. Setting her prices too high in order to compensate for this advertising expenditure could reduce the number of bookings for parties that the business receives so could reduce her revenue.

31. The business plan

1 B

2 C

3 A business owner will write a business plan to persuade lenders and investors to provide the start-up capital that they need. The business plan can be used to demonstrate that the business owner has researched their market and that the business is a viable venture that will not fail soon after launch. It also contains financial forecasts, showing whether the business is likely to provide a good return on investment or to make enough profit in order to repay the loan. Potential lenders and investors can then use this information to make an informed decision on whether or not to lend the money to the business and to assess the level of risk associated with the loan.

32. The nature of business planning

1 Having a business plan will be important for the success of Marcus's newly opened shops. Choosing Option 1 will help Marcus to make important decisions on factors such as pricing, advertising and layout. He will be able to do this based on the market research that he will gather and include in his business plan. The projected financial figures in his business plan will also help him to work out how he will repay the £30 000 loan and when his new shops are likely to make a profit. For these reasons, the plan will make it more likely that he will succeed in securing a loan, as it will show potential lenders that he is well-prepared and therefore a low risk. However, having a business plan does not guarantee success. There are many factors that Marcus cannot foresee, such as the actions of competitors and changing consumer tastes. Furthermore, Marcus is opening his new shops in the highly competitive city of London and it will be difficult for Marcus to anticipate how customers will react to his shops.
Overall, I believe that Marcus should choose Option 1 because a good business plan is important to the success of a business. While other factors are also very important, such as the quality of the food, a good business plan will consider these relevant factors, including quality, competition and product differentiation.

33. Stakeholders

1 A

2 B and C

3 i = G, ii = C, iii = H, iv = B, v = D

34. Stakeholder conflict

1 A

2 Possible answers include:
  • mine workers
  • BHP Billiton's customers
  • the Australian government
  • the local community in Queensland.

3 Possible answers include:
  • mine workers wanting higher wages and BHP Billiton's shareholders wanting higher profits and dividends
  • mine workers wanting more breaks per shift and mine managers wanting to increase the productivity of their mines
  • mine workers wanting higher wages and BHP Billiton's customers wanting lower prices.

4 A shareholder's key interest in a business is the amount of money that they receive in return for their investment. Conflict between other stakeholder groups, such as between employees and managers, may have an impact on the profitability of the business and therefore on the dividends that shareholders receive. For example, in the case of BHP Billiton, conflict between employees and managers over working conditions led to a strike, which the business expected to affect supplies to customers. This could have a negative impact on the business's reputation and therefore on the number of customers who choose to purchase supplies from BHP Billiton, which could reduce the business's profitability and the dividends received by shareholders.

35. Technology and business

1 Possible answers include:
  • email
  • Computer Aided Design (CAD)
  • Geographical Positioning Systems (GPS)
  • 3D printing
  • Electronic Point of Sale (EPOS).

2 One disadvantage is that employees have to be trained to use the new technology. This can result in lower levels of productivity while they learn, which might lead to a fall in profits if fewer products and services are sold as a result.

3 One example of technology that can have an impact on the marketing mix is social media. This is because a business may use social media to build its brand and communicate with its customers. In addition, a business may choose to use social media over other traditional advertising media such as newspapers and billboards because it is cheaper for the business. Social media means that promotion can also be done entirely by the business's own employees, rather than having to hire a PR agency or team. Social media also makes it much easier for a business to spread global awareness of its brand and products because people can repost tweets and images shared by the business, and this activity can reach a much wider audience. This also reduces the business's advertising costs as consumers spread the business's advertising on its behalf, rather than needing to pay for advertising space in lots of different places.

36. Principles of consumer law

1 Possible answers include:
  • Mixon's quiches must be good quality and edible
  • Mixon must disclose full information about the ingredients in its meals and drinks.

2 Choosing Option 2 will ensure that Mixon does not contravene consumer law by using misleading advertising about the weight-loss properties of its products and the quality of the ingredients that the business uses. Contravening consumer law could result in a fine or legal action by customers, and it will also have a negative effect on consumer opinions of Mixon's brand or brands. In turn, this could cause sales and revenue to fall. Even if the claims do not break consumer law, customers may consider it misleading, meaning that it could still have a negative impact on the business's reputation and sales.
On the other hand, the advertising claims about natural ingredients and weight loss may not be breaking any law. If Mixon's packaging contains full details of the contents of the products, it has complied with consumer law by disclosing all information about its products and allowing consumers to

compare nutritional information with competitors' products. In addition, these claims might be common in advertisements for similar products, meaning that consumers might not find them misleading, and choosing not to use such claims may put Mixon at a disadvantage in relation to its competitors.

In conclusion, I believe that Mixon should choose Option 2. Using the phrases in the case study could attract customers, but there is a large potential risk of angering customers who feel that they have been misled by the business's advertising claims, so it depends on the level of risk that Mixon is willing to take.

37. Principles of employment law

1 If a business adheres to health and safety laws, it is likely to operate in a safe working environment. This could lead to fewer accidents or injuries to employees, which might make employees feel valued and cared-for and could therefore improve employee retention rates.

2 If the government increases the minimum wage, a business may have to pay its workers more. This will increase its costs, which could lead to this cost being passed on to customers through higher prices. This could lead to a fall in demand for the business's products and services.

3 If a business does not comply with recruitment law, this may mean that it is discriminating against certain groups of people in its recruitment process. For example, a business that refuses to hire employees over a particular age because of their age is breaking the law. If the business is caught acting illegally, it could be prosecuted, which could lead to a fine or even to the closure of the business. Furthermore, failing to follow recruitment legislation could lead to a business having a bad reputation among consumers, employees and potential employees. This could reduce employee morale and could make it more difficult for the business to attract high-quality employees if the business is known to act unethically.

38. The economy and business

1 Consumer income is the amount of money that potential customers earn.

2 **B** and **E**

3 Rising consumer income is likely to result in higher demand for products and services. This might mean that businesses have to increase production by employing more workers. This increased production should meet consumer demand and lead to higher sales and increased profits.

39. Unemployment and inflation

1 **A**

2 Unemployment is the number of people who are unable to find a job but are willing and able to work.

3 Low rates of inflation will ensure that the prices charged by suppliers will remain quite low and will not rise sharply. This will allow a business to more accurately estimate its total costs in the future and will ensure that the business's cash flow remains healthy.

40. Interest rates

1 4.5%

2 **A** and **C**

3 Low interest rates help stimulate demand because they make it cheaper for people to borrow money. As a result, more people will take out loans to pay for things such as cars and extensions to their houses. This will then increase consumer spending and demand for products and services.

41. Exchange rates

1 **A**

2 An exchange rate is the value of one currency expressed in another currency.

3 If the pound becomes stronger against the US dollar, this means that buyers in the USA must pay more for the whisky they buy from the UK. As a result, demand for UK whisky will fall as some buyers in the USA may consider it to be too expensive or may wait to buy until the price falls. As less whisky is exported from the UK to the USA, the profit of whisky producers in the UK will fall. However, one option for whisky producers in the UK might be to lower their prices slightly in order to counteract the exchange rate to ensure they maintain their level of sales to the USA.

42. External influences

1 Possible answers include:
   * legislation
   * the economic climate
   * technology.

2 Changing legislation may affect UK businesses by making it harder for some businesses to trade. If a business makes a product that is subsequently banned by new legislation, then the business will not be able to sell that product any more. The business may try to expand its product range but could be forced to stop trading.

3 As more people are encouraged to use renewable sources of energy, such as solar panels and electric cars, this might provide an opportunity for businesses who provide these products or similar products and services. Furthermore, businesses may also develop their products to ensure that they use less energy or are produced in an environmentally friendly way, and are likely to use this in the promotion of their products. As more people are encouraged to be more 'green', the demand for this type of product is likely to increase. On the other hand, businesses may consider being pressured to use more renewable energy as a threat. In the future, it is likely that the government may choose to increase taxes on businesses and products that are not environmentally friendly or using renewable energy. This could increase costs for many businesses who fail to adapt to the use of renewable energy sources.

43–48 Theme 1 exam skills

1 Price low, customer involvement high.

2 £5500 × 1.08 = £5940

3 Knight Construction Ltd could use social media to promote the business, such as posting pictures of its building projects on Instagram or Facebook.

4 Using a market map allows Knight Construction Ltd to understand its competitors better, which helps the business to identify the USP of providing high customer involvement while charging lower or similar prices to competitors that offer much less customer involvement.

5 By becoming a private limited company, Knight Construction Ltd now has limited liability. This means that Cormac is only liable to the extent of the capital he invested in the company. As his business grows, this means that there is less risk of him personally becoming bankrupt if the business fails. Becoming a private limited company also gives Cormac the opportunity to take on new shareholders to invest capital into the business and become directors of the company. This is important as Cormac intends to expand his business and take on more employees, as it will give him access to another form of capital rather than having to rely on his own savings or borrowing from a bank.

6 This strategy enables Knight Construction Ltd to help its customers to manage their money more easily, which the business could promote as a USP. Market research could help Knight Construction Ltd to find out whether many customers would take this option when choosing a builder, and the business may find that doing this may give it Knight Construction Ltd a competitive advantage over rivals in the local area. Nevertheless, offering credit to customers can be risky and Knight Construction Ltd will have to pay for materials and labour up front whenever they begin a new building project. This could cause the business cash-flow problems on large projects, especially if some customers fail to pay by the agreed deadline.

7   By choosing Option 1 and making the business's website more professional, Knight Construction Ltd will support the promotion of the business. When customers visit the website, they will see that the company is professional and this will reassure them that they will get a professional service from the business. Furthermore, having a website that features videos of successful products means that customers can find out more about the company and the standards that it can achieve. This too will promote the business and build a strong brand image.

However, although the improved website will project a more professional image, it will not improve Knight Construction Ltd's marketing mix by itself. The marketing mix is also influenced by the way in which the business's employees communicate and deal with customers, which is a significant element of the Product element of its marketing mix. If employees do not do this effectively and achieve high standards on each project, the business's marketing mix will fail.

Overall, I think that Cormac should choose Option 1 because a good website is very important for modern businesses. Most customers will visit a builder's website before making a choice whether or not to give them a contract, and a professional-looking website will help to persuade them to choose Knight Construction Ltd. However, any advantage provided by Option 1 will depend on whether Cormac can ensure that other factors in the marketing mix are not neglected. A website will mainly help with promoting a business but many other factors are just as important to ensure an effective marketing mix.

8   Often building projects can exceed the initial quotation, meaning that many customers will worry about their finances when committing to a project such as a house extension or loft conversion. By doing its best to ensure this does not happen, Knight Construction Ltd will reassure customers, increase customer satisfaction and help to develop a good reputation in the local area. Many customers may choose builders through positive word of mouth and recommendations from friends, rather than through paid-for advertising or the business's online presence. By having highly satisfied customers, Knight Construction Ltd is more likely to attract new customers and grow the business.

However, it will not always be possible for the company to do this as it may run into unforeseen problems on any project, such as a rotting roof or problems with a building's foundations. Unforeseen issues encountered during a building project can result in costs rising. In addition, external influences, such as the economic climate and the cost of building supplies that Knight Construction Ltd purchases from its suppliers, are also having a significant effect on the business's costs, increasing them by 15%. If Knight Construction Ltd is unable to pass these costs on to its customers, its profits will suffer.

Guaranteeing to meet the quoted price is certainly a benefit to Knight Construction Ltd and its marketing mix, as price is a key factor for customers of building businesses. However, if the finished product is of a low quality, then customers will not recommend the business to friends and family and its reputation may suffer. This means that Cormac's decision may be a poor decision.

Overall, many customers will consider quality to be the most important factor when spending a lot of money on a new building and it is important that Knight Construction Ltd get this right before it tries to meet the budget set by a quotation. However, this may depend on the needs of the customer and the nature of the building project.

Theme 2: Building a business

The following pages contain suggested answers to the questions in Theme 2 of the Revision Workbook. In many cases, these are not the only correct answers.

49. Business growth

1   A takeover involves one business buying a majority of shares in another business so that it has control over the second business.

2   A business might want to grow because it has established itself and is successful. In this case, owners could want to grow the business because it has potential to increase its market share and therefore its sales and profits.

3   A business could grow internally by changing its products, perhaps to widen its product range or introduce improved products that are better than its competitors' products. This is likely to attract new customers, which will increase sales revenue and allow the business to reinvest its profits in order to grow internally. The reinvested profit could be used to open new stores or to enter new markets. Investing in extensive promotion could also encourage internal growth, because as the business builds its brand and spreads awareness it will attract new customers to purchase its products and services.

50. Public limited companies (PLCs)

1   Option 1 gives Snap the potential to raise considerable capital through selling shares to the public. If Snap succeeds in selling 15% equity, it could raise more than $3bn. This finance could then be used to develop its technology and spread the product around the world. However, becoming a PLC means that the directors of the business will be subject to the demands of shareholders who are entitled to a vote on key business decisions. Furthermore, the directors cannot decide who buys these shares or how the stock market price will change. If the value of shares falls in the future, so will the overall value of the business.

Option 2 (crowd-funding) may be successful as Snapchat is very popular. However, it is difficult to see what incentives or rewards Snap could offer potential crowd-funders. In addition, the popularity of the app might work against the business as crowd-funders might not understand why Snap chose crowd-funding when it has other options not open to smaller businesses.

Overall, I think Option 1 is the right choice for Snap. The app is very popular, so it is likely to be valued highly, and a stock market flotation will allow the business to raise substantial money and compete with other social media giants such as Facebook and Twitter. The success of the move will depend on whether the business starts to make a profit in the future. If it does not manage to turn a profit, its share price will inevitably fall.

51. Financing growth

1   C

2   Taking out a loan puts the business in debt, which increases the business's level of risk. The business will have to pay interest on the loan value, meaning that the amount of money it repays will be larger than the amount of money that it initially borrowed. It may be negatively affected by any increases in interest rates, as this could increase the amount of money that the business must repay to the bank. However, unlike share capital, loan capital does not involve giving anyone else control over business decisions, which means that the business may be freer to make its own decisions.

3   If Pret A Manger uses retained profit to finance its growth, the business is taking a much smaller risk because this method of financing growth will not put the business in debt. If Pret A Manger continues to expand into other countries such as the USA, this strategy increases the business's level of risk because it may not be able to adapt to local demand. This means that a low-risk method of financing this growth is even

more important to Pret A Manger. However, the business may not have enough retained profit to raise all of the finance necessary to open multiple shops in different countries, which means that the business may have to seek loan capital from a bank or raise additional share capital by issuing new shares.

52. Why business objectives change

1 C
2 The entrance of a new competitor into the market may mean that an existing business would need to amend its current objectives. For example, if the existing business had an objective to expand, it may now aim to retain its market share instead.
3 A business will set an objective to increase efficiency if it wants to improve its profits. A business that is efficient will use fewer resources and this will help it cut back on costs. If the business can maintain its sales revenue while also increasing efficiency, this strategy will help it to raise profits. Another reason might be to reduce waste and be a more sustainable business. A sustainable business can promote its products as environmentally friendly to increasingly environmentally aware consumers, which could attract additional customers and sales revenue.

53. How business objectives change

1 D
2 Market conditions can affect business objectives because they can create new opportunities. If consumer spending increases, a business may choose to increase its sales targets in order to maximise its sales revenue when there are higher levels of demand.
3 An objective to increase a business's product range could benefit the business by appealing to a larger number of potential customers. This would help the business to maximise its customer base and therefore its sales revenue. Selling a wider range of products may add value to the business's products, especially if the products are related or accessorise with one another, or it could enable the business to enter new markets and therefore increase the number of customers that it reaches.

54. Business and globalisation

1 A multinational is a large company with facilities and markets around the world, which often has a lot of influence.
2 Globalisation is good for an exporter because it opens up new markets to which it can sell. If an exporter can sell to more countries, then the demand for its products and services will rise and this will help to increase its profits.
3 Small domestic businesses might suffer from the process of globalisation. This is because globalisation gives people opportunities to buy goods and services from abroad, which might mean that small local businesses are not able to compete with large multinational companies who have the advantage of economies of scale. Globalisation could also benefit small businesses if it gives them the opportunity to sell their products online and ship them to customers in other countries. This means that they no longer have to sell to a small local market, but have the opportunity to attract foreign customers.

55. International trade

1 Operating within a trade bloc means that businesses in countries within the trade bloc can trade on favourable terms with other countries in the bloc. This means that the prices that they charge consumers in the other countries within the bloc are likely to be lower than those of businesses from countries outside the trade bloc, which gives them a competitive advantage.
2 A tariff is a tax imposed by a country's government and levied on imports into that country. If the UK puts a tariff on imports from countries like Kenya, then this is likely to reduce

demand for Kenyan coffee in the UK because its prices are likely to go up as a result of the tariff. This will reduce sales of coffee and may affect employment opportunities for people who work on the coffee plantations in Kenya. As a result, Kenya's GDP may fall and businesses may go out of business. However, Kenya may export much of its produce to other countries that do not impose tariffs on imported goods such as coffee. The Kenyan coffee growers could also look for new customers within other European countries or other nations in Africa. If they are able to do this, then a tariff imposed by the UK government may only have a limited impact on exports of coffee from Kenya.

56. Competing internationally

1 C
2 A business could change the ingredients in its products or the recipe for its products in order to suit the different tastes of consumers in other countries.
3 Using e-commerce to compete internationally allows smaller businesses to compete for customers in a global market. E-commerce allows them to sell to people in other countries without needing to undertake the risk and expense of opening stores in other countries.

57. Ethics and business

1 Possible answers include:
   • lobbying the government
   • creating negative publicity for bread producers that use misleading advertising
   • creating positive publicity for bread producers that produce bread that meets the Campaign's standards
   • advertising to raise consumer awareness of the impact of poor quality bread products.
2 Option 1 would help the Real Bread campaign to shame the businesses on the list into changing their practices in order to avoid negative publicity and any resulting loss of revenue. This is because these businesses may be concerned that consumers who are interested in the nutritional content of their bread will stop buying their products and start buying similar products from competitors who are not on the list published by the Real Bread Campaign. However, some of the producers on the list are likely to make a considerable profit from selling lower quality bread products and may feel that the publication of the list will have a minimal impact on their sales.
Option 2 is a more positive strategy, meaning that there is less risk that bread producers and consumers will react badly. Bread producers who would be concerned about losing business from concerned consumers may be very likely to work with the Real Bread Campaign in this way, as it could significantly improve the promotion aspect of their products' marketing mix. It could also attract new customers and could even reduce competitors' market share. However, it is less likely to have the same level of impact on producers of poor quality bread.
Overall, I think the Real Bread Campaign should choose Option 2. Naming and shaming businesses may cause negative publicity for the Campaign as well as for businesses, as consumers may feel that they are being lectured by the pressure group. Working with a bread producer to improve its products could raise consumer awareness of the issue just as effectively as Option 1, but it would do so in a much more positive way. Ultimately it depends on whether the Campaign wants to use a positive or a negative strategy, which is a decision that depends on the market research that the Campaign may have done into its target audience.

58. Environmental issues

1 Possible answers include:
   - using recycled packaging for their stationery
   - only using renewable sources of wood for their paper products
   - only using recycled paper
   - only using local paper suppliers to reduce their CO_2 emissions.

2 Paperclip might do this because it will improve its reputation for sustainability among its customers, many of which are businesses that may also have their own environmental targets to meet and so may be attracted to a more sustainable supplier.

3 Improving Paperclip's environmentally friendly business practices will help the business reduce its carbon footprint. This means that it is supporting sustainability and protecting the environment, which is a benefit to all aspects of the country and economy. Another impact might be that more ethically aware customers will choose to buy Paperclip products over the products sold by other office suppliers, especially if the customers are businesses with their own 'green' policies to comply with. This might give Paperclip a competitive advantage and result in Paperclip having a larger market share than rival office suppliers that do not follow the same policies or have not won recognition and awards for their environmental policies.

59. Product 1

1 The design mix is a model that considers how a business should balance the three aspects of aesthetics, function and cost when designing new products.

2 Unless a business focuses on function, its product is unlikely to do its job and therefore meet customer needs. This would result in the product causing poor customer satisfaction and being judged to be low quality, and large numbers of customers may choose to return the product for a refund.

3 It is important for a business to differentiate its products so that its products are unique and easily distinguished from those of its competitors. If a business's products are not unique, the business can only compete with rival brands on price, and lowering prices could have a negative effect on the business's profitability.

60. Product 2

1 B

2 An extension strategy is an approach a business would take to boost the sales of a product when it enters the decline phase of the product life cycle.

3 Possible answers include:
   - new packaging
   - rename the product
   - add new features or benefits
   - launch a new advertising campaign.

4 Using the product life cycle enables a business to decide when it is right to launch new products. If it knows that its products are reaching the decline phase, the business may use this as an opportunity to discontinue them and launch new ones. Another benefit of using the product life cycle is the fact that it allows the business to decide when and how new products should be promoted. A product entering the growth phase may be benefiting from increasing popularity, meaning that the business may not need to promote it as extensively as in Phase 1.

61. The importance of price

1 A and D

2 A business might want to increase its prices if its costs have increased. If its sales remain the same once the prices have increased, this will ensure that the business's net profit margin does not suffer as a result of the increase in costs.

3 Price is closely linked to quality in the marketing mix because price gives customers a perception of value and therefore of quality. If a product is sold at a premium price, this suggests to consumers that the product is a high-quality product. Some customers may purchase products with a high price for this reason. Alternatively, a low price may be considered to signify poor quality. Some customers may be put off by a low price because they believe the product will be of a low quality and will not fulfil their needs.

62. Pricing strategies

1 Introducing new technology in the production process can help a business to reduce its production costs. This may allow it to implement a different pricing strategy, such as penetration pricing, in order to gain a competitive advantage over its rivals.

2 Option 1 (lowering prices) would help Diva to achieve higher sales volumes, especially in the period leading up to Christmas. Many consumers spend heavily leading up to Christmas and offering lower prices would help the business to attract a bigger share of the market. This strategy may attract customers into Diva's stores if the price reduction is promoted heavily in the business's high street stores, which would help Diva to reverse the 5.6% decline in its in-store sales. However, this strategy may not be sustainable in the long term, and competitors such as Primark and H&M may simply reduce their prices in response.

Option 2 (increasing advertising) will increase Diva's total costs. However, it may help Diva to increase its sales and the proportion of its products that it sells, especially as sales volumes fell 2% on the previous year's sales. The associated increase in sales revenue may be enough to offset this expenditure. If the promotional activities are done well, they could also help Diva to build its brand image and potentially attract new customers to its stores, which could boost its in-store sales.

Overall, I think Option 2 is the best option for Diva. The business sells clothes in a competitive market, so it may already be selling at a low profit margin in order to compete with high street rivals such as Topshop, Primark and H&M. Ultimately, the success of the advertising campaign will depend on how well it connects with customers and encourages them to visit Diva's stores.

63. Promotion

1 C

2 A business might use social media because it is free. This means that the business can save this money and invest it in product development. As a result, its products will improve and be more desirable to customers.

3 A well-established business may choose to make cutbacks on its promotion because sales revenue has fallen. By cutting back on its promotion costs, the business could maintain its profit margin and maximise profit. Another reason for cutbacks on promotion may be that the business does not believe that the money it is spending on promotion is effective. Instead, the business may choose to use other forms of promotion or to do no promotion at all. This might allow the business to spend the money funding another business function, such as staff costs or product development.

64. Promotion, branding and technology

1 Possible answers include:
   - the ability to charge a premium price
   - increased consumer trust in the brand and its products
   - prime positioning by retailers.

2 A business could use its website to promote itself by ensuring that its website is attractive and easy to navigate. This means that customers will have a better experience when using it, and will visit the business's website instead of visiting and buying from competitors' websites.

3   Having the world's most valuable brand is a benefit to Google because it will help strengthen its balance sheet position and may increase its share prices. This will keep its shareholders happy and provide the business with a good means of raising finance, as more investors are likely to want to buy shares in such a valuable business. Google is already a well-recognised brand and market leader, so while overtaking Apple in terms of brand value may bring the business more short-term publicity, it is unlikely to improve its products or services. It also does not necessarily help Google to sell more of its products and services to customers, although the brand recognition associated with such a valuable brand is likely to help. The true value of a brand comes from the amount of trust that customers have in it. Apple's decline in iPhone sales shows that even the largest and most valuable technology businesses must keep up with customer needs and competitors in order to survive and succeed.

65. Place

1   C and E
2   The benefit of using e-commerce to sell products online is that there is no need to operate an expensive retail store. This means that the business can make savings on expensive overhead costs, which can then be passed on to customers through lower prices, providing the business with a competitive advantage.
3   A business might want to consider the cost of its proposed location in relation to the benefits of that location. This varies depending on the type of business. Having premises on a busy high street in a pedestrianised city centre may be very expensive, but the business is more convenient for passing trade. It may also increase customer awareness of its brand by being in that location. For other businesses, locating on an out-of-town retail park is better because it is often cheaper to rent or buy premises there. This is especially true if the business requires a large retail space, such as a large furniture business, or if its customers are likely to value ease of parking over high-street convenience.

66. Integrated marketing mix

1   An integrated marketing mix will help Samsung to market the Galaxy S8 and S8+ effectively to customers at the right price and through the right promotional channels. Samsung is recovering from the publicity surrounding the Note 7 and know that it is extremely important that the new products meet consumer expectations. As a result, its promotion focused on the features of its new products, communicating them effectively so that customers are reassured that the S8 and S8+ will not suffer the same problems as the Note 7. Despite this promotional focus, some customers may still have some reservations, but they may be enticed back to the brand by a new lower price.
     Nevertheless, an integrated marketing mix will not be effective if Samsung has not focused sufficiently on quality assurance in its production process. Quality assurance will allow the business to ensure that all phones meet and exceed customer expectations. If there are any quality issues with the new smartphones, Samsung's reputation may be damaged again, so it is important that it focuses on quality assurance as well as an integrated marketing mix. Estimating the level of demand for the new products is another important factor. This will allow Samsung to produce the correct number of smartphones for the launch, so that there is not a shortfall in supply. When a new smartphone is launched, demand is often high as customers rush to have the new technology. If Samsung cannot meet consumer demand for its product, customers may choose to buy a product from a competitor such as Apple or LG. Overall, an integrated marketing mix is very important and this is especially true for a business where the product has had negative publicity in the past. Nevertheless, there are many other operational issues that a global business must

also get right if a new product launch is to be successful, so the success of the products depends on the way in which Samsung manages these other factors as well as its marketing mix. I would suggest that Samsung ensures the quality of the new product is excellent by implementing extensive quality assurance before releasing the new smartphone.

67. Business operations and production

1   Possible answers include:
     • hire more staff
     • introduce new technology into the production process
     • change the type of production process used.
2   One benefit of batch production is that it allows a business to add variety to its product line. This means that it can produce more products to meet a wider range of customer needs and this will help it increase sales by attracting a broader range of customers.
3   Flow production allows a business to standardise its products. This means that every example of one product will be the same, ensuring that customers can rely on the business to provide the same quality product every time they purchase from it. It also allows a business to save costs on employees, as it can employ less skilled employees at lower wages than it would require if it used job production. Flow production also has limitations for businesses, such as the fact that it can be very expensive to purchase and set up the required machinery. It is also less flexible than other production methods, such as batch production.

68. Business operations and technology

1   Introducing new technology could improve a business's operations by reducing human error. Machines are more consistent than humans so they are less likely to make errors, such as cutting something to the wrong length. This improves the product quality and reduces the number of faults.
2   A business could increase productivity by using automation. Automation involves using machines and computers in flow production. This means that a greater number of standard items can be produced in a shorter space of time without having to increase the number of employees or inputs.
3   As a business's machinery gets older, it becomes less efficient and might need to be repaired. When machinery is being repaired, there is downtime when production stops because the machinery cannot be used and there is no output. Another factor affecting productivity is the motivation of the workforce. When employees feel demotivated as a result of reasons such as low pay or poor working conditions, they are less productive because they feel unhappy. This results in productivity falling because employees work at a slower pace and do not feel committed to the business.

69. Managing stock

1   20 models.
2   Stock arrival date (6 weeks) – reorder date (4 weeks) = 2 weeks.
     OR
     Stock arrival date (10 weeks) – reorder date (8 weeks) = 2 weeks.
     OR
     Stock is ordered in week 4 and arrives in week 6, so 6 – 4 = 2 weeks.
3   One benefit of just-in-time stock control is that it helps a business to keep its fixed costs low. This is because a business needs to have enough space to hold large amounts of stock, and this can be expensive. Lower fixed costs will improve the business's cash flow, meaning that it is better equipped to meet any unforeseen costs.
4   Holding large amounts of stock could help Cara and Cole to cope with unpredictable surges in demand for their dinosaur models or increases in demand at certain times of the year, such as at Christmas. This is because it ensures that Cara and Cole have enough stock to meet demand and will not run out.

It also ensures that Cara and Cole are unlikely to lose out on sales due to problems in the supply chain, as they might do if there were delays to the just-in-time delivery of their dinosaur models. Holding large amounts of stock can take up a lot of space, even if the models are not assembled immediately, and Cara and Cole may need that space to store assembled and painted models that are ready to be sold.

70. Suppliers and procurement

1 D
2 One reason is the flexibility of the chosen supplier. Often, demand changes over time and the business needs to meet the differing needs of its customers. If its supplier is flexible in terms of its products, resources and delivery timing then this will help the business adapt to changes in the market and continue to generate enough sales to survive.
3 An unprofessional supplier could fail to deliver stock on time. This could result in customers not receiving their goods on time. This could damage the reputation of the business and lead to negative customer reviews, bad publicity and negative word-of-mouth. Furthermore, an unprofessional supplier could also be providing goods and resources that are of low quality. This means that the business will also be selling or producing products that are of low quality. If the quality of its products does not match the prices that it charges for them, customers will not buy the products or will be dissatisfied and return them. This too could damage the business's reputation and lead to a fall in sales.

71. Managing quality

1 When a business is known to offer high-quality products and services, this adds value to its products and services. This means that they have a higher value and are worth more to customers. As a result, customers will be more willing to pay a premium price for them.
2 Option 1 is a good option, as quality control can help a business achieve high quality standards because it involves a process of checking the standards of products so that no faulty TVs leave the factory and are delivered to customers. As Werther has launched a new TV with new technology, there is a higher chance that there may be some faults. However, although quality control will ensure no faulty products go out to customers, it does not necessarily mean that there won't be faults.
The benefit of Option 2 is that quality assurance involves focusing on quality at each stage of the production process. This will involve all employees being trained in quality processes. If everyone is involved in quality, then there is less likelihood of any faults, although developing quality assurance systems may be expensive and take time to put in place.
Overall, I think that Werther should choose Option 2. Quality assurance is the best of the two approaches because it will help Werther to build a culture of quality where quality is a part of everyone's roles, but this may depend on the resources that Werther has available to ensure that quality assurance has the investment required to make it work. As Werther operates in a very competitive market where technology is constantly improving, quality may be a key factor in how Werther competes with rivals such as Panasonic, Samsung and LG.

72. Customer service and the sales process

1 C
2 Possible answers include:
   • customer interest
   • speed and efficiency of service
   • customer engagement
   • post-sales service
   • customer loyalty.

3 Option 1 should be relatively easy for RightOnTime Cabs to implement, as it already has an informal policy of never being more than 2 minutes late. Using a guarantee in promotion could also show customers that the business values its customer service greatly. As RightOnTime Cabs specialises in airport transport, many of its customers will need to get to their location at a certain time, and reliability is one of the key factors on which customers will base their choice of taxi business.
Option 2 is a good option because it will encourage repeat custom. This means that the business could start to build a base of regular customers in the north-east of England who are loyal to their brand. However, the discount has to be large enough to undercut the prices of the eight other taxi businesses in the area in order to be attractive to customers. If the discount has to be quite large, this strategy could affect the business's profit margin.
Overall, I think that RightOnTime Cabs should choose Option 1. This option shows a commitment to providing good customer service and will help the business to improve its customer service. This is a good strategy because many customers will use the taxi service again and recommend it to other people if the service that they receive is good. This is important for a taxi business, for which it is difficult to differentiate the service that they provide. This is especially true for RightOnTime Cabs because of the number of competitors in their local area. Improving customer service will help RightOnTime Cabs achieve a competitive advantage if all other local businesses fail to meet this customer need, but in the long term good customer service is unlikely to be a unique and defensible strategy for the business.

73. Gross and net profit

1 B
2 Gross profit is the profit that a business makes on its trading activity before any indirect costs have been deducted.
3 Net profit = Gross profit − Other operating costs
Net profit = £200 − £115
Net profit = £85

74. Profit margins and ARR

1 Net profit margin (%) = $\frac{\text{Net profit}}{\text{Sales revenue}} \times 100$

Net profit margin = $\frac{£14\,750}{£30\,000} \times 100 = 0.49166 \times 100$

Net profit margin = 49.17%
2 Average rate of return (%) =
$\frac{\text{Average annual profit (Total profit / No. of years)}}{\text{Cost of investment}} \times 100$

Average annual profit = $\frac{\text{Total profit}}{\text{No. of years}}$

Average annual profit = $\frac{£700\,000}{5}$

Average annual profit = £140 000

Average rate of return = $\frac{£140\,000}{£400\,000} \times 100 = 0.35 \times 100$

Average rate of return = 35%

75. Interpreting quantitative business data

76. The limitations of quantitative data

1 Possible answers include:
   • a product that improves effectiveness of exercise
   • a product that improves healthiness of diet
   • a product that integrates with social media
   • a product that monitors medical conditions
   • a product that controls household technology
   • a product that controls entertainment technology.
2 A recommendation by their doctor.

3 Wearable technology such as smart watches is a technology that will support the healthcare industry by reducing costs. As customers use the technology to monitor their health, they will consciously take action to improve it, such as taking more exercise or visiting their doctor when their blood pressure is high. This will allow the healthcare industry to put in place preventative measures to prevent serious issues such as diabetes, obesity and heart attacks. As these conditions are more successfully prevented, hospitals will spend less on curing them and their costs will fall. Many healthcare businesses will also see wearable technology as an opportunity to make money from consumers who are conscious about their health and well-being.

4 Qualitative data provides a business with an understanding of its customers, including their attitudes towards and opinions of the business's products and services. This information can help a business to improve its products in order to meet its customers' needs. Quantitative data includes sales data and profit margins. This data can tell a business that it is not performing as it had hoped to perform, but it does not help the business to understand the reasons behind this. Furthermore, quantitative data such as statistics can be misinterpreted, especially if the statistics are not representative of the whole population. Using both quantitative and qualitative data together allows a business to see trends in sales data while also using customers' opinions to understand those trends and to take action to resolve any problems.

77. Organisational structures

1 C

2 A hierarchical structure is a business structure that has a long chain of command and multiple layers of management.

3 Possible answers include:
- to delegate decision-making to parts of the business that understand the needs of local customers
- to motivate employees and make them feel valued and respected.

4 A benefit of centralising decisions is that the business will be able to ensure that all of the decisions are being made in line with company policy. Another benefit is that it allows the business to ensure that individual managers are not making decisions that cause their individual part of the business to fail. However, centralising decision-making may mean that the decisions that are made do not consider the specific issues faced in different parts of the business. It could also make employees feel less valued and respected, because they do not feel that they are trusted to make good decisions. Furthermore, if managers in various parts of the business have previously had autonomy in their decision-making, taking this away from them may damage their morale.

78. The importance of effective communication

1 Possible answers include:
- use of jargon in instructions to bakeries
- human error when distributing changed ingredients lists to bakeries.

2 Communication is especially important for a business such as the CrustCake Bakery, which has 30 small bakeries across the south-west region. This is because products will be made in each individual store, but they all need to look and taste the same if the business is to build a trusted and reliable brand. Furthermore, the owners of CrustCake Bakery will also need to receive accurate feedback on customer needs and opinions. Tastes may be different in different parts of the region and different cakes may sell better in one location than another. It is important that this information is communicated if the business is to adapt to local needs.

Although communication is important, other factors are also significant. Having a large number of small bakeries will be very expensive to run, so it is very important that the business

is able to manage the overheads across the 30 locations. For this reason, cash flow will be just as important to the success of the business as the communication within the business. Overall, communication is very important because it will help all employees to feel as though they are part of a larger organisation and not just an employee in one small bakery. Furthermore, in order to create a consistent brand, the business's decisions, recipes, displays and signage need to be coordinated, and this also relies on good communication. Nevertheless, improving communication will be pointless if the business is not financially secure, so the business may need to prioritise other factors before it can focus on communication. When it does commit to improve communication, it is important for the business's managers to set up effective channels such as newsletters, events and meetings where employees from different bakeries can come together to share ideas and discuss issues.

79. Different ways of working

1 One benefit of part-time employees is that it helps a business adapt to customer needs. If demand increases, a business can take on more workers to meet this demand. A business can also reduce its labour costs when there is a lull in demand, which allows a business to control its costs more effectively.

2 Freelance contract employees are not permanent employees and may be brought in to complete a certain function for a business, such as a business consultant who specialises in a certain aspect of business. This allows a business to access these specialist skills only when it needs them instead of having to employ someone with these specialist skills full-time. This allows a business to manage its labour costs more effectively.

3 One technology that can be used to improve the way people work is an intranet system. An intranet system allows a business to store important information such as customer details, internal systems and policies in one place. The intranet is secure and password protected so that employees can access this information securely from any location. This means that employees do not need to operate from one office and could work remotely from anywhere in the country or even the world. Intranet technology therefore allows people to be far more flexible in the way they work as they can work from home or while they are on the road visiting customers. Employees can also access these systems at any time of day, which allows employees to work flexible hours at times of day when they are most productive.

80. Different job roles and responsibilities

1 B

2 Possible answers include:
- director of holiday sales
- head travel agent (supervisor/team leader)
- travel agent (operational staff).

3 One responsibility of a manager in a business is to carry out performance management of subordinates. This involves setting targets and monitoring performance. This role will help ensure all employees are working productively, which will contribute to the overall success of the business.

81. Effective recruitment

1 A business would want references to ensure that the potential recruit is telling the truth about their experience and skills. A referee could confirm the roles that a candidate has completed and comment on their skills and attitude towards work. This will help a business ensure it is recruiting the right person for the job.

2 A person specification outlines the essential and desirable characteristics of a recruit. This document will help a manager shortlist applicants. Once applicants have been shortlisted, the person specification provides a set of criteria against which each applicant can be evaluated. This will support the selection of a candidate with the right qualities for the role.

3 Using external recruitment will allow Colin to increase his workforce and bring a new person into the business who is an expert in adventure holidays. This will help him to move into the adventure holiday market without having to use a freelance adviser, which could be more expensive in the long term. Furthermore, external recruits will also bring new ideas into the company and add their own experience to the team. External recruitment can be costly and it takes time for new employees to settle into the business before they are fully productive and integrated. By choosing not to use internal recruitment, Colin is also missing the opportunity to promote one of his current employees, which could improve employee morale and demonstrate that there are promotion opportunities in his business.

82. Developing employees

1 Performance management helps businesses to achieve their aims. This is because employees' targets are linked to those of the business, so monitoring and reviewing employee performance against these ensures that all employees are performing to the desired standard and helping the business achieve its aim.

2 Option 1 will help Philip's mechanics to develop the skills to upgrade cars' on-board computers. This will not only improve the skills of these employees but also ensure his business can provide additional services to customers as well as standard services such as MOTs and engine repairs. This will add value to the service that AutoSure provides. This will help generate additional income streams for his business, which will contribute to its overall profitability. Furthermore, the mechanics sent on the training course will feel as though they are being invested in and this will increase their morale. Nevertheless, formal training courses can be expensive and Philip will be losing his workers while they are training. This could result in an inability to carry out fewer MOTs and repairs required to break-even.

Option 2 could help to enrich senior mechanics' jobs by giving them additional responsibility for training junior mechanics. It is also cheaper than sending his mechanics on a formal training course, but Philip cannot guarantee that all junior mechanics will be trained to the same standards.

Overall, I believe that Philip should choose Option 1. Investing in formal training is good for a workforce and will ensure that AutoSure and its mechanics are able to keep up with the latest technology and developments in the industry. This is important if his business is to be competitive. However, the usefulness of investing in the training depends on whether Philip can guarantee the quality of the training provider before sending his employees on the course.

83. The importance of training

1 Self-learning is usually done on employees' own time and may involve accessing training courses online rather than going to a training centre. As a result of this, the business will not lose employee productivity during the working day. This means that there is less chance of revenue falling as a result of training employees.

2 One benefit of investing in training is that it can help improve motivation in the workforce. Employees will feel that they are valued and that the business is investing in their skills, and this will make them feel happier and willing to work harder. This improves their productivity and output.

3 Training employees to use new technology can help improve the efficiency of and communication within a business. It can also ensure that the business is keeping up to date with the latest developments in the industry. As a result, there is more chance that the business will remain competitive and may even gain a competitive advantage over its rivals. Introducing new technology can also cause problems as employees need time to learn how to use new software or machinery. During this learning period, there is more chance of productivity falling and of mistakes being made.

84. Motivating employees 1

1 B

2 Possible answers include:
- fringe benefits, such as a company car
- paid overtime
- bonus scheme
- commission.

3 One disadvantage of paying workers by the hour is that the business cannot expect them to complete tasks beyond their working hours in order to meet customer needs without paying them overtime, such as when a job or project overruns. Overtime can be very expensive because employees often expect it to be paid at 1.5 or 2 times their hourly rate.

4 Paying employees using a bonus scheme may encourage them to work harder in order to achieve the targets that will help them secure a bonus payment. This motivation to achieve the financial reward will help the business to attract and meet the needs of more customers. For a bonus scheme to work, the business must consider how the system will work for different types of employees. For example, operational staff may have a different bonus system to supervisors or team leaders. This is because these employees have very different roles and will have to be measured in a different way in order for the system to work.

85. Motivating employees 2

1 Possible answers include:
- avoid losing staff to competitors such as Starbucks and Costa
- improve employees' morale and customer service to compete with rivals such as Starbucks.

2 Carltens could introduce job enrichment by giving employees the opportunity to make key decisions in their individual café and take on greater responsibility for menu choices.

3 Introducing an employee reward scheme such as employee of the month will ensure that Carltens' employees feel that they are being recognised for their hard work. It will also improve the self-esteem of employees who receive the reward, which is important as self-esteem is considered a key contributor to motivation. The scheme may also encourage competition between workers who strive to gain the status and recognition associated with receiving these awards. However, competition between employees is not always healthy and it can lead to some employees choosing not to co-operate with others in order to achieve the reward themselves. Similarly, some employees, such as those who do not win, may not care about the reward scheme. As a result, some of the workforce may not be motivated by or benefit from the scheme.

86–91. Theme 2 exam skills

1 Between 2011 and 2016, there was a growth trend in the market for new cars.

2 If the car manufacturing industry is well-established in Austria, Jaguar may choose to manufacture its cars there because it will be easier for the business to hire qualified employees and work closely with suppliers.

3 Net profit margin (%) = $\dfrac{\text{Net profit}}{\text{Sales revenue}} \times 100$

$\dfrac{255\,000\,000}{65\,500\,000\,000} \times 100 = \dfrac{255}{65\,500} \times 100 = 0.3893 = 0.39\%$

4 Jaguar employs around 40 000 people in the UK alone. To organise this number of employees effectively, Jaguar will need to divide them into a number of divisions, each of which will have its own organisational structure. This is because Jaguar is a global brand and part of the multinational company Tata Motors, which means that Jaguar may be part of a hierarchy that is already very tall. In addition, controlling so many employees may require many layers and roles such as head of engineering and manufacturing team leader. Within this structure, Jaguar's employees are likely to have clearly defined job roles, which may mean that they are likely to specialise in one thing such as car design or automotive engineering. However, this structure may also provide opportunities for promotion, which may help boost morale and create job satisfaction.

5   Receiving industry awards such as Best Executive Car will help Jaguar to attract lots of positive free publicity. This helps the business to promote its products and its brand, and it contributes to its already established brand image. Customers may value and pay attention to these awards as they are awarded by impartial experts in the industry, rather than being seen as advertising created by Jaguar. Many customers may then be inclined to buy a car from Jaguar on the basis of the brand's status and the high quality associated with the award. Another benefit is the internal impact that receiving awards will have on the business's engineers, designers and sales staff. The recognition and self-esteem of contributing to the success of the business in winning these awards can be a motivating factor, as many employees will feel pleased to be associated with this success. High levels of motivation can lead to higher rates of productivity and employee retention.

6   Option 1 could improve the sales of Jaguar's electric car by making consumers aware of the fact that the well-known luxury brand is offering a new and different product. This may boost Jaguar's sales and revenue, especially at a time when purchases of new cars are increasing as shown in Figure 2. It may also attract new environmentally friendly customers who may not have bought a Jaguar in the past but who are more willing to purchase an electric car from the luxury brand. However, increasing promotion activities will increase Jaguar's total costs, which may offset the increased revenue from the additional sales revenue that the promotional activity generates.

Option 2 is quite an unusual tactic for a car manufacturer like Jaguar, which may mean that it could attract a lot of media attention and therefore free publicity for the I-Pace. This means that this option could be a cheaper way of generating the same additional promotion as offered by Option 1. However, it would be a risky strategy and the cost of even a limited product trial with a high-value car may be so large as to make this strategy impossible to undertake. A limited product trial is also likely to be of little use as it can only convince a relatively small number of Jaguar's potential customers, whereas increasing advertising will reach a far larger group of potential customers.

Overall, I believe that Jaguar should choose Option 1. Increasing consumer concerns about the environmentally friendly nature of the products that they purchase should ensure that the I-Pace attracts a lot of positive consumer interest, and the strategy is relatively low risk. Option 2 could be an interesting and eye-catching strategy, but it is unlikely to significantly improve sales of the I-Pace as the trial would have to be very limited.

7   Entering the electric car market will bring Jaguar a number of benefits. The first is that consumers are becoming more environmentally conscious so more people are turning to electric cars such as the Tesla. As the market continues to grow, more car manufacturers will be encouraged to develop their own range of electric car and it is important that Jaguar does not get left behind. Furthermore, it is important for all businesses, especially car manufacturers, to keep innovating in order to encourage customers to buy new cars rather than sticking with their old cars or buying second-hand cars instead.

However, Jaguar is better known for its high-powered luxury sports cars like the F-Type, and many of its loyal customers may see this new approach as a move away from the business's strengths and brand heritage. Similarly, many environmentally conscious consumers may choose not to buy a Jaguar electric car because of the brand associations with luxury and speed.

The danger is that Jaguar's current brand image may be a barrier that prevents it from breaking in to the electric car market. Another drawback is that many other manufacturers such as Smart and Nissan have had electric cars on the market for a number of years. This means that they already have a first-mover advantage over Jaguar as well as the competitive advantage of an existing and loyal customer base of consumers who want to purchase electric cars.

Overall, it is a good idea for Jaguar to enter the electric car market at this point. Figure 2 shows that the new car market in the UK is growing, so this is a good time for Jaguar to expand. In addition, electric cars are more sustainable and, in the long term, Jaguar may have to invest in this technology for all its products, so it is better to do it now rather than waiting for its profits to improve before taking the risk. However, the success of this move depends on the way in which Jaguar manages its brand image as it moves into the electric car market. As the I-Pace is going to be marketed as an electric sports car, it may struggle both with brand loyalists who want to buy luxury cars and with ethical consumers who want to buy sustainable cars. Because Jaguar has a strong brand image, its loyal consumers will trust any new model that the business launches. However, Jaguar's marketing for the I-Pace must convince these existing customers that they want to buy the I-Pace, even though it may be quite different to Jaguar's other products, such as the F-Type.

Notes

Notes

Notes

Notes

Published by Pearson Education Limited, 80 Strand, London, WC2R 0RL.

www.pearsonschoolsandfecolleges.co.uk

Copies of official specifications for all Pearson qualifications may be found on the website:
qualifications.pearson.com

Text and illustrations © Pearson Education Ltd 2017
Typeset and illustrated by Kamae Design, Oxford
Produced by Out of House Publishing
Cover illustration by Miriam Sturdee

The right of Andrew Redfern to be identified as author of this work has been asserted by him in accordance with the
Copyright, Designs and Patents Act 1988.

First published 2017

21 20 19
10 9 8 7 6

British Library Cataloguing in Publication Data
A catalogue record for this book is available from the British Library

ISBN 978 1 292 19070 9

Printed in Slovakia by Neografia

The author and publisher would like to thank the following individuals and organisations for their kind permission to
reproduce copyright material.

Photographs
Reuters: Lucy Nicholson 86

All other images © Pearson Education

Notes from the publisher

1. While the publishers have made every attempt to ensure that advice on the qualification and its assessment is accurate,
the official specification and associated assessment guidance materials are the only authoritative source of information and
should always be referred to for definitive guidance.

Pearson examiners have not contributed to any sections in this resource relevant to examination papers for which they have
responsibility.

2. Pearson has robust editorial processes, including answer and fact checks, to ensure the accuracy of the content in
this publication, and every effort is made to ensure this publication is free of errors. We are, however, only human,
and occasionally errors do occur. Pearson is not liable for any misunderstandings that arise as a result of errors in this
publication, but it is our priority to ensure that the content is accurate. If you spot an error, please do contact us at
resourcescorrections@pearson.com so we can make sure it is corrected.